The 21 Day Miracle

How To Change Anything in 3 Short Weeks

Table of Contents

How to Get Anything You Want

Do you want to know the biggest lie in personal growth?

The Tortoise and the Hare.

You've been told that slow and steady wins the race. And you've been told that persistence and consistency create champions.

They don't.

That's because in real life, the rabbit *always* wins.

Always.

Want proof? Put a *real* rabbit next to a *real* turtle in a *real* race. The rabbit smokes the turtle every time. Vegas won't even give it odds. No one bets on the turtle—he's consistent, persistent, and very, very slow.

This morning my son cornered a rabbit in our garden. "Hey Dad, I have this rabbit trapped. Come check it out." Three seconds later, the rabbit was through the fence and sprinting about 1,000 miles an hour down the driveway.

Rabbits are fast.

Which brings me to you. Has it ever dawned on you that you're a rabbit surrounded by turtles? For years they've been trying to box you in, contain you, and slow you down. They even tell you this ridiculous story about how turtles beat rabbits.

Listen carefully: **you were meant for more.** You have a message, story, or experience that's going to change the world. And I didn't need to tell you that. You've known it all your life.

Problem is: you haven't gotten to your dreams yet.

Imagine for a moment what it would be like to have the power to accelerate your success. Imagine having the tools to make your dreams a reality. Imagine being able to change anything in your life and to have total control over your mind, your body, your emotions, your relationships, and your future.

Imagine what it would be like to finally get out of debt, get in shape, make a pile of money, and then smile, breathe, laugh, fly, and soar.

You haven't achieved this yet because you've been told that "slow and steady wins the race."

You've been told a lie.

According to a recent study,[1] only one person in three reports being happy. Think about that for a moment. It's strange when you consider the world we live in. Push a button and you get a ride. Push a different button and you get food. Push yet another button and you get music, movies, and entertainment.

Two hundred years ago, water was scarce. Today we go to the *bathroom* in water.

How is it possible that in light of so many luxuries, so many people are unhappy?

Answer: because they're rabbits in a world ruled by turtles.

What if you could invest just three short weeks to become the person you want to be? What if you could quickly accomplish your goals and simultaneously increase your income and impact? What if you had a secret formula for accomplishing any goal—no matter how hard?

You'd win every time.

This book is about winning. Every time.

Part I—The 21-Day Miracle Manifesto

There is a scene in the movie *Amadeus* where the King tells Mozart that his symphony has "too many notes." The King has horrible taste in music so Mozart replies that his symphony has "just as many notes as are required, neither more nor less."{2}

And he was right. He was, after all, Mozart.

So at the risk of comparing myself to the greatest composer of all time, I'll share my rule when it comes to writing: "neither more nor less." In other words, this book is exactly how long I want it to be—and not very long at all. I find no need to pad it with quotes, graphs, stats, or long-winded narrative.

For your sake (and mine), I'll get right to the *point*.

The fastest way between two points is a straight line and so my goal for you is simple:

1. I want you to read this book.
2. So you can implement what is in this book.
3. So you can move on to the business of changing the world.

Thusly,[3] this book is both short and to the point.

Also, I am not a scientist and this book is not based on “science.” I know that comes as a shock—“science” being the god that it is. But my reason is simple: scientists *watch* things and attempt to predict the future.[4] I want to be the kind of person that *makes things happen* and changes the future.

So, except for the stray statistic or footnote, this book is built on actual real-life experience won on the battlefield of Planet Earth.

Oh—and while I am on the subject, I am not a relationship expert or a fitness expert, nor am I a lawyer, accountant, or investment advisor. Nothing in this book should be taken as advice on any of the above.

I am, however, pretty good at flying an airplane at insane speeds and I know how to explode just about any business (in a good way).

So you should take my advice. (If you are reading this on an eReader, be sure to read the footnotes. I am not sure how those shows up on your device, but you'll miss a lot if you skip those.)

This book is arranged in three Parts.

Part I contains everything you need to launch your own 21-Day Miracle and see magnificent results. Here you'll learn the secret to a "strategic sprint," how to create your own destiny in short bursts, how to plan your victory, and how to overcome any obstacle along the way.

Part II breaks down the 10 most common 21-Day Miracles and shows how to implement them. We'll cover everything from mind mastery to weight loss.

Part III contains the 10 most common 21-Day Miracles outlined in succinct plans you can execute now.

You can implement everything in Part I without Parts II and III. But you *can't* do *anything* in Parts II or III without Part I. If what I just said doesn't make any sense, then start right here and read straight through. If you jump ahead to one of the "Tools of the Trade" chapters in Part II, you'll end up lost and confused, and you'll blame me.

Plus, when you read from here all the way to Part II, you'll discover a little surprise that won't make any sense unless you cover the ground in Part I. No one likes ruined surprises.

So flip the page. It's time to change the world.

Defying Gravity—The Secret to Not Being Normal

Consistency is for losers.

And it doesn't work for at least half of us. In fact, it doesn't work for nature either. Take a look at just about anything in the real world and you'll see that nature, from teens to watermelons, grows in fits and starts, sprints and stops, struggle and rest.

There's a reason why you have a long trail of gym memberships behind you. You signed up and planned on hitting the treadmill every day for the rest of your life. Now the membership card burns a hole in your pocket while the memory burns a hole in your conscience.

Let me be the first to tell you—it's not your fault.

You were not created for a "lifetime" gym membership. You should have gone there for three months—at the most—then moved on to another activity that sparked your interest and fanned new flames of ambition.

So I'll kick off this chapter with a single principle that will dominate this book...

The Most Successful People Design Their Lives Around "Strategic Sprints."

Take, for example, fighter-pilot training.

Back in 1996, I left the frozen tundra of Quantico, VA[5] (Marine Corps infantry training) for the sunny beaches of Pensacola, FL (Navy flight school).

It was there I learned the value of strategic sprints.

In ground school, a young student learns physics, engine mechanics, emergency procedures, flight rules, meteorology, swimming, first aid, and land survival.

It would take the average civilian flight student a year (or more[6]) to cover these topics.

The Navy does it in a single 3-week sprint.

Open mouth.
Insert fire hose.

Turn on.

Repeat.

It was at Navy flight school that I first discovered the difference between successful people and everyone else. Successful people compress time and do things faster—not because they can but because they realize *everyone* can. And this realization that "everyone can" enables them to do what to many seems impossible.

Did you catch that? This secret isn't available to the elite few. It's available to you, me, and the village idiot.

I should know—I failed Kindergarten. And I still went on to graduate from Top Gun, fly in combat, and become one of the leading instructors in the F-18.

You've been led to believe that the first lesson in goal setting is to "set realistic goals."[7] That's total baloney. Whoever invented that was a Turtle. You should throw that piece of advice out your car window. And then drive over it a few times just to make sure it's dead.

Who cares about doing something "realistic," "normal," or "possible?" Henry Ford once said that if he had followed conventional wisdom he would have "invented a faster horse."

I succeeded in life because I set completely unrealistic goals, convinced myself that I could achieve them, and then I did. And why not? After failing Kindergarten, I only had one place to go. Up!

Back to the Navy. The "unrealistic" pace doesn't end at ground school. During flight training, the Navy's model is as follows: Teach, Demonstrate, Do.

And it all makes perfect sense to everyone—except the student.

Teach

The young student sits admiringly while his instructor draws a perfect landing pattern on the whiteboard. The student nods his head to demonstrate that he understands completely. He doesn't. He is lying. He has no idea what the landing pattern looks like (other than that strange oval on the whiteboard). He's never even flown an airplane. So he continues nodding and taking notes as the instructor teaches with the gusto of Patton in the opening scene of—well—*Patton*.

Demonstrate

The young student sits in the backseat of a raging tin can full of fuel, oil, and ambition. He[8] is told to "watch and learn" as his experienced instructor flies a perfect "pattern"—descending, lowering the flaps, and slowing to a perfect speed while "greasing" his precise landing with the formulaic agility of a Russian ballet.

"Got it?" the seasoned instructor asks his student (who is now slightly airsick).

"Yes, sir. Got it." This is the student's second lie and they're adding up now.

Do

It is now the student's turn. He is perched in the front seat of the raging tin can full of fuel, oil, and ambition. He carries a legacy of Naval aviators with him spanning back before World War I. He tosses his scarf[9] over his neck, throws caution to the wind, and readies himself for his first real landing. He is, after all, the second coming of Iceman from *Top Gun*.

And then, with his heart set on flying a perfect landing pattern, the young student promptly tries to crash.[10] With youth and enthusiasm, he tries, in vain, to kill himself multiple times. It's then that he discovers that he has literally no idea how to fly and that he is a danger to both himself and the local town. The young pilot is repeatedly seized out of the jaws of death by the wise and experienced instructor in the backseat who, in the process, saves countless lives and millions{11} of dollars in government property.

The student doesn't know any better. For this young man, so full of hope and honor, has lied. He has no idea what he is doing.

So much for Iceman.

And yet, despite the lies, the failure, and the near-death experiences, in just three short weeks, our young student is flying alone on his first solo flight, at speeds that would shock the average man.

Three weeks.

How was this transformation accomplished?

Simple: it was a strategic sprint with a single (and "impossible") purpose. For three full weeks, this young buck{12} inundated himself with thoughts about the landing pattern. He woke early and went to bed late, mentally asking for "clearance to land." He learned to trust his instruments, to fly upside down, and to handle any emergency.

He didn't know any better. Every other pilot ahead of him learned to fly in three weeks, so he could too. And in just 21 short days, he is no longer a danger to himself or others.

He is a pilot.

Now back to you.

Have you ever started something, only to get frustrated and give up? Do you have a legacy of attempts and mistakes? Do your friends and family simply roll their eyes in a mocking glow at your next stab at certain failure?

Welcome to the club. The only difference between you and the young Navy pilot is this: this young man *had* to become successful.

And so do you.

So, if I may be so bold, when would be a good time to get going in the direction of your dreams?

How about now?

You can start by doing this: First, shed the idea that your life, goals, or ambitions have to be *normal*. Then, set a somewhat ridiculous and unrealistic goal. And finally, create a "sprint" that gets you *one step* closer to your goal. I'll show you how in this book.

Here is my most recent "sprint": a book, a website, and a video training—all in 21-Days.

This thing you're reading right now is the book.{13} I am currently halfway through Day 1 and I've written 3,000 words. Not half bad, especially since I type like a chicken on amphetamines.

Most people think it takes three years and a cabin in the woods to write a book.

Successful, fast-moving rabbits can do it in three weeks. In fact, most of the writing for this book will be done in four days or less.[14]

The website part of this project is where you can go and get a free training. I'll start on that next week. Most web projects take months (maybe years). This one will take me three days or less.

The training product will be a series of videos showing you how to execute what's in this book. Most products are the result of light years of planning, outlining, and scheming. I'll knock it out in two days.[15]

How can I do all this in three weeks?

Simple: big goals and big focus. No email. No texting. No Facebook-Distraction-Time-Suck. Just writing, recording, and creating.[16]

In the following pages, I'll show you how to create big objectives and hit them every time through a process called the

21-Day Miracle. It's nothing more than a focused 3-week "strategic sprint" that will get you closer to your grand future.

But before I do that, I want to tell you about the time I didn't eat for 21-Days.

"That's Right, Iceman, I am Dangerous"

Everyone has their weakness.

I'm sure you've heard that phrase a thousand times. You may have even told it to others. And the fact is, it's partly true. There are some things you weren't created to do. {17}

That said, the little phrase above can be used and manipulated by the Turtles of the world to slow you down.

Take something like food.

Food is a wonderful gift from God. It tastes amazing and makes you feel all happy inside. Even thinking about food can get you excited. It's a beautiful social blessing that gives us all a reason to sit down and enjoy one another.

But much like anything, food can control you. *Everyone has their weakness* should not apply here. You should not be a slave to food. Unfortunately, I was.

I loved food. I appreciated food. I honored food. And then I stepped over the line and food started to "own" me. Now—just like you—I have big dreams and big ambitions. I have a certain amount of strength and I plan on using it to changing the world, not dreaming about my lunch.

So, in an effort to take some mastery over my appetite, I went to an age-old approach to controlling food—not eating at all.

As in at all—at all.

I spent an entire 21 calendar days consuming nothing but water.[18]

For three days, I was hungry. Really hungry.

Then on the fourth day, my physical hunger dissipated, leaving an emotional "Gee I really miss my old friend food" hunger.

I remember driving by Taco Bell and having an emotional "Gosh I really miss Gorditas" reaction. The bizarre thing is, I never eat at Taco Bell—ever. I've never had a Gordita. Not once. So it wasn't my stomach talking. My mind simply imagined a pretend love affair with the slop Taco Bell puts on their slop.

It was then I realized the power of the brain. My love for food wasn't an actual physical need for anything. The people who study water fasting will tell you that after three days, your stomach and hunger go into hibernation. It was all in my head. My brain (and a bunch of stray thoughts and emotions) were trying to dictate the very direction of my life.

And in 21 short days, I had all that control back.

Was it hard? You bet it was. Hard enough I would never recommend anyone start fasting with 21-Days. Start with a meal, then a day, then three days, then try the whole thing.[19]

By the time I was done, I was in charge of my brain, my belly, my thoughts, and my impulses. The result of my 21-Day fast spread into the corners of my life. I realized if I could conquer food, I could conquer money, fitness, relationships, and personality.

The results surprised even me.

Conversations that would have bothered me a month before just came and went. Difficulties that would have had me stressed out just didn't.

I was, as they say, a different man. The grass (literally) looked greener, the sky bluer, the clouds sharper. All as a result of 21-Days spent doing (or in this case not doing) something.

I had discovered the holy grail: **21-Days of focusing on *one* thing can completely transform *everything*.**

And the best part is the results spread into other areas of life. Gaining mastery over one thing made it infinitely easier to gain mastery over the others. My thoughts begin to submit and obey. They stopped running the asylum and started doing what I told them to do.

Armed with the secret to fixing nearly anything, I set off to overcome my next obstacle: fear—fear of the unknown, fear of finances, fear of people's opinions, and for that matter, every other kind of fear.

Oprah once said that when we do something, we are only and ever motivated by one of two things: love or fear. I wanted to be motivated by love, not fear, so I set out on a 21-Day Miracle to crush fear.

I got that and more.

To beat fear, I went completely off the grid and away up into the mountains. I left my computer at home, sent my phone to my assistant, and travelled from San Diego to the Rocky Mountains using a road atlas.[20]

For 21-Days I hiked, fished in rivers, camped (sometimes), built fires, and generally connected with God and nature. Some days I got rained on. Other days I got sunburn. Some days I fished and caught nothing. And on other days I caught (and released) the most beautiful brown trout ever seen by man.

Some nights I stayed in a cabin and ate barbecue, elk burgers, and popcorn. I had no schedule, no place to go, no deadlines, and no agenda.

My only goal was just to be (and not be distracted while I was *being*).

If someone wanted to get ahold of me and they called, texted, or emailed, they got a response from my assistant in California. I was, for lack of a better word, *gone*.

Sounds amazing, doesn't it?

It was.

But do you want to know a secret? For the first five days, I was so terrified I almost quit and went home.

Seriously, do you know how difficult it is to just let go of everything? I have a family, a couple of businesses, a bunch of training products, and about 40 clients. The moment I drove out of town without any connection to the world, I began to worry about the most extraneous things.

One morning I woke early enough to be the first person to complete the 3-mile hike up to the Delicate Arch in Moab. (It's such a crazy-beautiful creation that the state of Utah put it on their license plates.)

Just as I crested the hill and caught sight of the sun coming up over the arch, my mind went sideways and I thought, *Someone just died—you need to go back home now.*

I tried to talk some sense into myself, but my brain kept going. "This is serious. Maybe someone did just die. Maybe something really bad just happened. Here I am taking in a nature hike while real people are struggling. Gosh this is selfish. Maybe I should just go home."{21}

In the midst of this mental battle, I reminded myself what I had come out here to conquer: my inner voice wanting to spread fear and panic into an otherwise clear mind.

So I fought back. I stayed. I prayed. I found a nice little spot and took a nap. I thanked God for the sunshine, the rocks, the birds, and the trees. I thought about all the good things and for the peace of being disconnected.

And I won.

21-Days later I came home to a perfectly healthy family and a stronger mind. So powerful was my breakthrough that, once completed, I could scarcely remember what I was afraid of before I left. Money issues? Relationships? Health? Why did those things ever bother me?

I had no idea.

As with my 21-Day water fast, a lot of unexpected benefits came along as well.

Being gone (ironically) helped my business. That's because, in order to survive without an owner, a business has to have real "systems" in place. Most business owners don't have a system. They have themselves. And when they are gone, their business falls apart. Being gone forced me to create systems in my business before I left. They are still in place today.

Another side benefit of being gone: relationships were set right. I can't explain how this works, but you and I both know how some relationships can get out of line after time. Take clients, for example. I've had over 350 one-on-one coaching clients from all walks of life including large franchises, famous speakers, authors, and movie stars. As a consultant, you are in charge. You have to be. If not, the client won't see the kind of results they want.

But somehow, over time, I let some of these relationships slip. Instead of being in charge, I was the one at the whim of the client. Maybe it was fear. Whatever the reason, 21-Days off the grid set all those right.

The last (and perhaps most important) benefit was regaining total mastery over media. Have you ever accidentally left your phone at home? You know that feeling of panic at being disconnected from the world? When you purposefully disconnect yourself for an extended period of time, all that goes away and you gain a right relationship with your phone. It is there to work for you, not the other way around. You're supposed to control it. It's not supposed to control you.

In other words, your phone can and should be turned off for long periods of time. When you do, it sends a message to your phone and to the rest of the world—you are important and you're not to be interrupted.{22}

Now, admittedly, the two stories I just told you are a bit extreme.

The good news is the 21-Day Miracles that I'll outline in the coming chapters are something you can do, very easily, bite by bite.

I am not going to ask you to fast for 21-Days or disappear into the mountains, so chill. You can do this on your terms and on your timing. This isn't a cult. You can pick and choose what to implement and when to tackle each challenge. In fact, one of the first things I'll show you is a way to totally control your mind so you *know* what to pick and when to do it.

Whatever happens, what you are about to read will show you how to take your life back and start living on your terms.

I know you may be getting excited about what's really possible for you, but if there is still a small voice of doubt in the back of your head, don't worry—I've got you covered in the next chapter.

The Ancient Secret to Changing Anything

I discovered something wildly unexpected and very helpful in Marine Bootcamp that will help you stay the course in your own 21-Day Miracle. The normal "stay" at this luxury resort is 13 weeks. The average American shows up an undisciplined bag of gnats and leaves a steely eyed warrior who can kill with his bare hands.{23}

But do you want to know how long it *really* takes to make a Marine?

Three weeks.

Three weeks to rule them all, Three weeks to find them,
Three weeks to bring them all and in the darkness bind them
In the land of Quantico where the Shadows lie.{24}

Here is the process: it takes 3 Days to break you, 14 Days from the start to obliterate any old habit patterns, and 21-

Days from the start to make you a full-fledged member of the pack.

The rest of the time is designed to hone, tone, and sharpen you. And to teach you how to shoot a bad guy at long range.

I showed up for my obligatory Boot Camp training with vigor, bravado, and confidence. *They might break the others, but they won't break me.*

I was wrong. It took three days for them to break me.

Contrary to public opinion, the first day at Boot Camp is *not* when the hell begins—it's more like the calm before the storm. On Day 1, you fill out a lot of paperwork, get about 1,000 shots, and get prodded by someone who calls themselves a "medical professional." It was during that first day that I had a conversation with Wilonski.[{25}] He was a candidate[{26}] like me, except this was his second try at Boot Camp. The prior year he had accidentally broken his toe and had to leave in the first week.

On Day 2, hell began. Talk about yelling. These guys could have used a course in anger management. Pack this. Move that. Faster. Too slow. Run. Run. RUN! You couldn't please these guys. Nothing worked. They were just plain old mad—and bent on staying that way.

It was at this precise moment that I realized I had just made the single worst decision in my entire life.

While all my college buddies sat on the beach drinking Natural Light, I was jammed into a stuffy Marine barracks getting yelled at by a cranky bald guy with halitosis. As regret began to pour in, I remembered my conversation with Wilonski and a thought began to form in my mind.

If I kick the wall as hard I can and break my toe this will all be over.

As a bonus, were I to execute my purposeful toe-destruction with vigor and completeness, the Marines would just chalk it up as an accident and I wouldn't be labelled a "quitter." In a few days, I'd be out on that beach, Natural Light in hand, telling stories about my two solid days in Marine Corps Boot Camp.

So I stood there for what felt like forever looking at my toe and then the wall.

And then I didn't do it.

I decided I would give it one more day. For, after all, you can break your toe anytime you want. What you can't do anytime you want is see what happens on Day 3 at Boot Camp.

That next night, I thought about breaking my toe again. And the night after that. And after a few weeks, I was feeling like a Marine and I never thought about it again.

The first principle I learned from almost purposefully and forcefully breaking my toe…

When it comes to accomplishing your dream, you don't have to do it all at once.

Take today as today and do today what you can do today. Forget tomorrow. It's a long way from now and not that important. As a very wise Man once said, "Tomorrow will worry about itself. Each day has enough trouble of its own."[27]

Here is the second principle…

The thing you thought was hard eventually becomes easy on the other side of implementation.

For me, Boot Camp actually became fun. I know that sounds strange, but I actually grew to like it. Just like that, in 21-Days I was a member of the pack and reveling in the joy. I was a kid again, running through the woods with a gun and shooting the bad guy.[28]

Even the physical fitness got to be downright enjoyable. 8-mile run? No biggie. I'm game. I am, after all, a Marine.

Which brings me to my third principle…

Once you decide to stick with something, the results show up. You just need to hang around long enough to get them.

There is a great story in the Bible about a very wise Presidential cabinet member named Daniel—someone who (also) fasted for 21-Days.[29] On the last day of his three-week fast, an angel showed up and said, "At the *beginning* of your requests, a message went out, and I have come to declare it to you, for you are greatly esteemed." In other words, the answer was sent the moment he started his 21-Day Miracle, but he received the answer at the end.

Know what would have happened if Daniel quit halfway through? Nothing. Which is why persistence is key. And heck, it's only 21-Days. You could stand on your head and spit nickels for 21-Days.

It turns out, 21-Days is the perfect time period to accomplish almost anything. It's long enough to replace old habit patterns with new ones. And it's short enough that you can see the light at the end of the tunnel.

For example, I am currently in the midst of one full alcohol-free year. Five years ago, this would have seemed impossible. So I started slow and took 21-Days off booze. Then, I took three months off. Now I am up to a year. It's not that alcohol is intrinsically bad—or that I had a problem. It's just that I want to be in charge.

The point is to start off slow. And 21-Days is the perfect combination of long enough and short enough. So let's get on to the process that will change your life starting now.

The 21-Day Miracle

Having laid the foundation, we now move on to how to actually change anything in 21-Days. It starts with a very simple process that has been around in one form or another for eons.[30]

1. State your desired result.

This first step is vital. It's where you get crystal clear on what you want to accomplish. I recommend using the present tense.

Before I started my 21-Day food fast, I created this statement to define my desired result:

> *I am in charge of my belly, my thoughts, and my impulses.*

Notice I stated my desired result in the present tense—as though it had already happened.

For my Rocky Mountain tech fast to eliminate fear, I created this statement to define my desired result:

I am motivated by love, not fear,

Very clear and, again, stated in the present tense.

Here are other examples of things you might state for your desired result.

- I have total mastery over my mind.
- I have total mastery over money.
- I am a warrior. I stand up for what's right and no one can stop me.
- I am in charge of my time and my schedule.
- I am happy and full of joy despite my circumstances.
- I look great. I am at my ideal level of fitness and I eat healthy food that I love.
- I have uplifting relationships filled with love, empathy, and protected with proper boundaries.
- I have written a book, created a website, and launched a video training

called the 21-Day Miracle.
- I am totally and completely free from being addicted to alcohol.

Once you've identified your desired result, it's time to do something with it.

Good: Write it down.

Better: Write it down and then say it out loud.

Best: Write it down, say it out loud, and then post it somewhere you can see it every day.

Better Than Best: Write it down, say it out loud, post it somewhere you can see it every day, and then tell the world that for 21-Days, this is what you're going to do.

Listen, there is something magical that happens with accountability. Your excuses fall away and your persistence doubles.

2. Associate a strong emotion to your desired result.

This second step is vital to crossing the finish line. You have to actually see, hear, and feel what it's going to be like when you accomplish your goal. People process emotion in three different ways: visual, auditory, and kinesthetic. You either see, hear, feel, or some combination of these three. So be sure to anchor your desired result with the kind of image you best respond to.

If you are a visual processor, associate your desired outcome with perfect *pictures* in your mind's eye. For ideal health, *picture* your ideal body in your imagination. For money mastery, *picture* yourself doing a leisure activity you love with the money you've earned. For business mastery, *picture* the kind of impact your wealth will have on the world.

If you are an auditory processor, associate your desired outcome with *hearing* the things you want to *hear*. For ideal health, imagine *hearing* friends and family saying how much you've changed. For money mastery, imagine people *asking* how you were able to do it so quickly. For business mastery, imagine *hearing* the crowd roar as you take the stage at TED.

If you are a kinesthetic processor, then associate your desired outcome in how you would *feel*. For ideal health, imagine how your body will *feel* after a really healthy meal. For money mastery, imagine the *feeling* of relief you'll have when you are out of debt. For business mastery, imagine how great it would *feel* to impact millions of lives with your product or message,

Most people are a combination of all three, so mixing and matching is totally cool.

Before I started my 21-Day "Water-Only Fast," I pictured myself being totally free from any addiction to food. I imagined myself having lost 30 pounds. And I imagined the feeling of accomplishment.

For my Rocky Mountain "Tech Fast" to eliminate fear, I pictured myself being totally free from fear about money, relationships, or the opinions of others. And I imagined how great it would feel to be the "Inner Warrior" I wanted to be.

Back to you. Last thing—smile.

I mean it. I want you to actually grin from ear to ear while you are saying these statements. Smiling make you happier and that means you'll get more done. The act of actually smiling tells your brain that whatever you're promising to do will give it endorphins.[31] It's a clever side-door hack into a brain function that flat out works. And really, you look so much better when you smile, so just do it, ok?[32]

3. Create the plan and take action.

Now that you've created the result and associated it with some kind of emotion, it's time to get down to the business of planning your attack.

I'll get to some specifics in the chapters that follow, but here are some general guidelines.

Make your plan realistic.{33}

Have you ever run in a 5k race and seen what people do at the starting line when the gun goes off? They take off like bats out of hell. It's hysterical. Hundreds of people running as fast as they can. You'll see them again—they'll all be on the side of the road at mile 2 because they used up their tank in the first 200 yards.

Take fitness. The reason most people fail is because they start too fast. They sign up for CrossFit, go every day for a week and then never go again.

So make your plan realistic. If your goal is mind mastery, maybe you can start with ten minutes of meditation a day. Easy. Then build on that to create more aggressive goals.

Keep your life and schedule in mind.

Your 21-Day Miracle should not consume your every waking minute. For example, I already shared that I am in the middle of a 21-Day sprint to write a book, create a training product, and launch a website. At this very moment, I am two hours into Day 2.[34] I wrote all day yesterday (Monday). And I will write most of the day today, tomorrow, and Thursday.[35] Friday, however, will be my weekly prayer day. It's one day I set aside every week for prayer, reading, thinking, and meditation. No email, text, social media, or writing.

Saturday is an editing day and then hanging with the kids: baseball, swimming, and relaxing. Sunday is church, brunch, and a nap. Monday is back to work.

The point is that life does not stop. You just insert a new pattern into the life you already have.

The next three short chapters are carefully designed to ensure you succeed with your own 21-Day Miracles. I'm going to tell you in advance where the challenges might pop up, and show you how to persevere through them.

Insider Secrets For The 21-Day Adventure

Remember when I told you ALL pilots make it through three-weeks of flight school insanity because they know all the pilots before them successfully passed? Here is a little secret I didn't tell you back then. One of the reasons they do so well is because their buddies in the previous class share their best strategies for success. It's a little bit of "military intelligence" that gives them a head start. The new students get a major benefit from knowing *exactly* what to expect.

I am about to do the same thing for you.

The 21-Day Miracle is the perfect combination of enough time to replace an old habit pattern while short enough to see the light at the end of the tunnel. That said, there is a typical pattern that most people experience, so we might as well just get it out into the open.

Days 1-3: The Challenge

The first 3 Days are the hardest. In fact, most of the real work happens right here at the beginning. The good news is while these are the hardest, they won't *feel* like the hardest. That's because you'll be riding a wave of excitement that has the power to propel you to Day 4.

In these first 3 Days, just remind yourself that you don't *really* need to do the whole 21-Days. You just need to do **today**. You can always quit and break your toe on the wall tomorrow. But today, you'll persist. Once you do that, you'll find yourself at Day 4 where the real work begins.

On Days 1-3, you'll also internally question this book and me. You'll tell your friends I am great, but secretly wonder if I made all this up to sell more books. If you review this book during Days 1-3, you'd give it 3 stars out of 5. Reluctantly.

Days 4-7: The Urge

This is when most people quit—right in the middle of week 1. While Days 4-7 are not the hardest days, they certainly *feel* like it. During these days, you'll be accosted and tempted by both your Inner and Outer Critics and you'll want to give up and move on. Plus, you'll think this process probably won't work anyway.

It's right here in Days 4-7 that you'll probably hate me, this book, and everything about it. You'll regret that you told your friends about it and you'll send me a long email that says "THIS DOESN'T WORK!!" in all caps and with multiple exclamation points. You'll probably ask for a refund on Amazon and post a "level-headed" (but nasty) 1-star review of this book.

I'll reply to your email by asking, "How long have you been at it?" And you'll sheepishly tell me it's 4, 5, 6, or 7 days, you were having a "moment," and that you'll stick with it, and delete your Amazon review.

Day 8-14: The Pendulum Swings

You've been at this for a week and you actually feel a lot better. You're seeing results and this is starting to work. The world hasn't exactly changed yet, but you know you're getting there. And better, you are starting to see that you have a tool in the 21-Day Miracle that you can use to change a lot of other things in your life too.

Your biggest challenge during Days 8-14 is thinking you've achieved a result when you haven't. The temptation to quit isn't because *this isn't working* but because it is. You'll want to take what you have and move on to something else.

Don't do it.

You committed to 21-Days. Finish the 21-Days. Remember, your results are on the way, but haven't arrived yet. Stick around long enough to get your results.

4-star review.

Day 14-21: The Momentum

By Day 14, your old habits are gone. Long gone. The only thing left is a small, faint, critical voice in the background that you can go ahead and just disregard. You'll feel great and you'll be surprised that it was ever that hard. In fact, you'll be surprised that *anything* was that hard.

You see the light at the end of the tunnel and you'll start planning your Day 22 Celebration.

5 stars, but tempered by an unenthusiastic "this book really helped me" review.

Day 22: Celebration

You did it. And you should be proud. You have done what no one in today's culture does—you've taken charge of your life and replaced one habit with another. Plus, you now have a tool and the confidence to use it.

Your book review is now a solid 5 stars and a glowing review with ALL CAPS and multiple exclamation points!!!!

Two thoughts for Day 22. First, celebrate. You owe it to yourself to have a blast and really enjoy this day. Do what you like: eat an expensive dinner, buy yourself something nice, watch a movie, go for a bike ride, or take a long walk. Seriously, go ahead and open the good bottle of Bordeaux.{36} You deserve it. As an added benefit, celebration will solidify the new pattern in your mind as something that is both to be desired and appreciated.

Second, give yourself some time before planning your next 21-Day Miracle. Your temptation here will be to immediately use this great and powerful tool to do something else amazing. Not so fast. Give it at least a week. Rest is a valuable part of this pattern and, between you and me, you could use a little break. Take the next week to smile (a lot) and scheme a new sprint (a little).

Last thing, when it comes to your own 21-Day Miracle, give yourself some grace and patience. You may fail. You may not do it perfectly. You may make mistakes.

It's been said that, "You'll treat everyone else's heart the same way you treat yours." So treat your heart with kindness and empathy. An imperfect 21-Days is better than no 21-Days. And the fact is, you'll have both Inner and Outer Critics trying to stop you along the way.

So let's just take the surprise out of their tactics right now, shall we?

Public Enemy #1—The Inner Critic

There are two things that get successful people off their game. Ironically, the first and most insidious adversary isn't anyone. It's a voice called the "Inner Critic."

Let's face it—your inner voice likes things the way they are. For years, he's[37] been in control and he likes it that way. He's been able to cajole, manipulate, and coerce you into being "normal." And for your part, you've listened and been a good little soldier. If your inner voice wanted you to be anxious, you became anxious. If your inner voice wanted you to quit something, you quit. If your inner voice wanted to sabotage your success, you joined in and sabotaged along with him.

The problem is, you're not normal—at least not anymore.

You're—you. And you were made for more. Plus, you're reading this book. So your Inner Critic is now acutely aware that you've spotted him. He's losing control. He's not happy. And he just heard me talking about him—again! So right now—at this very moment—he is coming up with some new ways to get you off your game plan.

The strategies he'll use is to get you to stop reading this book:

This is probably just psycho-babble, personal growth mumbo-jumbo. You've tried this stuff before and it didn't work.

This is an easy one to counter. Just keep reading. There is some good stuff coming. In fact, in a moment I'll tell you why most of your family members are broke and out of shape.

This isn't working.

The Inner Critic will try this tactic from the beginning of your 21-Day Miracle all the way up until about Day 10. You will be tempted to think that nothing is happening, that nothing is working, and that you were foolish to think anything would change. And this voice will grow even stronger if you happen to slip up and fail during the 21-Days.

The counter to this attack is to remember that the results come at Day 21 and after. So if the scale isn't moving, you don't feel amazing, and you're not "seeing" results, you have one choice and only one choice: keep at it.

You're doing it wrong.

The Inner Critic tried this on me for a solid week during my 21-Days away in the mountains. I kept having this sneaky feeling that I was doing it all wrong, that I was messing up, and this was a gigantic waste of time.

Here is the irony: I was there to do *nothing*. There was no agenda other than to *be*. How could I do that wrong?

It got so bad that on Day 10, I decided to head home. I figured I had accomplished everything I needed to and, after all, I was probably doing it all wrong anyway.

But instead of going home, I told the Inner Critic to shut up.

And having persisted, on Day 21, I received the idea for this book. As I was driving home, the entire plan for the book, the training product, and the website just popped into my head, almost like a reward.{38}

This won't last.

This is one strategy the Inner Critic can and will use for the entire 21-Days (and even after). He'll tell you that while you made some strides and accomplished some things, the results will never stick because *results never last for you.*

He'll remind you of your attempt-and-fail quest for fitness, good nutrition, money-making, and everything else you've aspired for. He'll show you all your defeats—that trail of tears spanning back years. He'll tell you that you're a nobody—to leave success to those who really deserve it.

Here is the counter for this move. Remind yourself that everything, even the failures, have made you a better, smarter, and faster person. Remember that success is like a spiraling staircase. Even though it feels like you keep coming back to the same spot, you've been climbing higher and higher, seeing the same things from a different vantage point.

Keep climbing. You're going to make it—and when you do, the world will never be the same again.

I liked it better the other way.

This last lie is probably the main reason people are unhappy, out of shape, or broke. You'll make strides and start to change. But when you experience resistance, the Inner Critic will lie to you and say that it was better when you were unhappy, out of shape, or broke. The Inner Critic will remind you of all the friends who are also broke—and how complicated life would become if all of a sudden, you had gobs of money and they didn't.

The counter to this lie is to bring yourself back to the desired result and the emotion you'll experience when you achieve what you want to achieve. Remember all those good things you imagined happening at the end of your 21-Days? Remind yourself of them over and over and over again.

Listen, you are in charge.

You're in charge of your mind, your will, your emotions, and your outcome. You can do whatever you want and you don't have to listen to the lies anymore.

When the Inner Critic starts to raise his ugly head, just say, “thanks for sharing,” and move on.

Eventually the fog will clear. Eventually the battle will be over. Eventually you’ll reach your goal.

Eventually you’ll win.

Eventually you’ll take complete control and the Inner Critic will die a slow, painful, and lasting death.[39] And many years from now, having accomplished your great big dream, you’ll wonder, *what ever happened to that voice?*

Because it will be gone.

Public Enemy #2—The Outer Critic

I'll get right to the point.

The majority is almost always wrong.

Most people are broke, lazy, and stupid. Most people who buy this book never read it. Most people who start it never finish it. Most people who finish it never do what's in it.

Most people vote for a candidate because of some stupid reason fed to them intravenously by the media.

Most people watch too much TV. Most people don't read enough books (or any).

Most people think they are independent. Most people aren't.

I have a phrase to describe most people. I call them "Hive-Minded Lemmings." They hang out with the hive, think like the hive, and behave like the hive. They believe whatever the hive believes without actually thinking or asking any questions. Then they jump off the cliff with the hive because they blindly believe the hive is always right.

Bzzzzzz.

Do you want to know how to identify a Hive-Minded Lemming? Just ask them one question, *any* question, after they state their belief in *anything*.

Take climate change. Ask someone (anyone) if they believe in climate change. Once they say, "of course" ask them one follow up question, *Which of the climate models do you think most accurately reflects what's happening with the environment?*[40]

See the frantic shifting of the eyes back and forth in the hope that the Queen Bee will give them the answer?

See the eventual blank stare?

Hive-Minded Lemming.

Here is another example. Just a few chapters ago I quoted the Bible and called it "good history." At that point, I usually have a bunch of people tell me how the Bible has a bunch of contradictions, was written a long time ago, and basically can't be trusted.

Bzzzzz.

I usually ask them, *What has given you the impression in your recent reading of the Bible that it has a bunch of contradictions. Or perhaps just show me one or two places in the Bible you think are contradictory.*

See the blank stare?

Hive-Minded Lemming.[41]

Now pay very close attention here: that person is decidedly not YOU. You were made for more. You're supposed to change the world. You have a mission, a purpose, and a plan.

You may have fallen into Hive-Mind thinking from time to time. So what? I have too. But let's agree on this together. From here on out, you'll think for yourself. You'll go against the majority and do what's hard. You'll persist to the end and accomplish what you have been put on this earth to accomplish.

It will be difficult and you'll face a lot of criticism. And that is very, very good news. Especially when you follow a very simple principle from a very Old Book: "Narrow is the way that leads to life."{42}

I am being very direct for an important reason: once you set out on your goal of changing the world, you're going to encounter resistance. The bigger the goal, the stronger the resistance. It's going to happen so you might as well prepare for it now. Start reinforcing the bulwarks and preparing for an attack so when it comes, you can just laugh it off and move on.

The first and most difficult of the "Outer Critics" to face will be the ones closest to you: parents, spouse, siblings, and friends. Just because they are close doesn’t mean you have to go with their opinion. And just because they are family doesn't mean they’re not wrong.

For years, Bronnie Ware—an Australian nurse and counselor—worked in hospice counseling and interviewing the dying. She asked hundreds of people within days of their death the same question: *What regrets do you have?*

Do you want to know the #1 answer (by a long shot)?

Here is it is—in their own words...

I wish I’d had the courage to live a life true to myself, not the life others expected of me.

Bronnie Ware goes on to say, "This was the most common regret of all. When people realise that their life is almost over and look back clearly on it, it is easy to see how many dreams have gone unfulfilled. Most people had not honoured even a half of their dreams and had to die knowing that it was due to choices they had made, or not made."[43]

It's enough to make you cry.

Some of the most magnificently strong people I have ever worked with get pulled down by some of the biggest losers on the planet (many of whom just so happen to be family members).

Listen—Outer Critics don't get a vote. There's only one vote in your life and it's yours. Sure, get advice. In fact, get a lot of it.[44] But not from Hive-Minded Lemmings. Take advice from people you trust who have walked your path with success.

For example, here is general rule that I have lived by since I started my business...

I don't take business advice from broke people.

Catch that? You can copy and paste it and create a new set of rules for yourself. Something like…

- *I don't take fitness advice from out-of-shape people.*
- *I don't take life advice from unhappy people.*
- *I don't take sales advice from people who can't sell.*
- *I don't take ______ advice from _______ people.*

I decided long ago that I could choose only one option from the list below:

- Option #1: I can live up to other's expectations.
- Option #2: I can live up to my own expectations.

That goes for everything, including expectations about life, career, money, parenting, relationships, food, and fitness. You can't serve two masters and there's a good, solid case to be made that you're a very good master and you can be trusted.

The great irony is that in trying to live up to everyone else's expectations, you will fail to meet *both* their expectations and yours. But sadly, most people live their entire lives trying to live up to some version of a themselves that someone else has in mind.

Your expectations are better.

Enough of the opinions, advice, and "help" of Outer Critic Hive-Minded Lemmings. They're all slow-witted Turtles. Starting now, you're going to go get what's coming to you, with no regrets. The world needs you so get on with it. You can bet that as soon as you start on your first 21-Day Miracle, you're going to encounter some resistance from the Outer Critic.

Just say "thank you for sharing" when the Outer Critic speaks and move along. You have a lot to do and not much time to do it.

Which brings me to my next point. Everyone on Planet Earth rides a roller coaster: you, me, and the gal down the street. At any given time, you can ride only one roller coaster. Choose wisely. Given the available options, ride yours. It's more fun—and frankly, yours has controls.

A year ago, I wrote 16 rules for my life. Here is Personal Rule #3:

> *I choose not to ride anyone else's roller coaster. Friends, bosses, spouses, colleagues, and clients will all go up and down. One minute happy; the next minute sad. One day hopeful; the next day hopeless. One week optimistic; the next week pessimistic. They have chosen to ride their own roller coaster—and often without any tangible reason as to why. It's my choice to get on. So I choose not to.*[45]

While I am on the subject of roller coasters, here is the one thing that can get you off yours and onto someone else's: their opinions. The thing that makes this so insidious is that it will sound like they are trying to help. In fact, most of the time they really do want to help. But when push comes to shove their "opinion" is going to get you off track.

From this day on, I give you 100% permission to disregard the opinions of anyone, even if you can't explain why.

I appreciate your opinion and I thank you for sharing. That said, I am going to go ahead and do it anyway.

Get help from good-hearted people who have walked your path and have the scars to prove it. Not only will they help you, but their advice will come from real life experience in the real life trenches.

Now that you know about the Hive-Minded Lemmings, their expectations, opinions, and snares, I have a final piece of advice.{46}

Have fun.

Smile.

Laugh.

A lot.

It hardens the good habits and eliminates the old.

And who knows? Along the way, you might just convert a few Hive-Minded Lemmings. They might start thinking for themselves and changing the world in their own way.

And many years from now, lying on your deathbed, you'll grin from ear to ear knowing you did it your way...

...and the world will never be the same.

Part II—Tools of the Trade

"You don't have to read the rest of this book," said no author ever.

But guess what? That's exactly what I am about to tell you. Simply put, you covered the ground you needed to cover. And you closed the gap between what you want and how to get it.

You know what it takes to create your own 21-Day Miracle. You know the process, the outcome, and the obstacles. The most important thing you can do right now is come up with a plan and implement it.

That said, I have a few more tricks up my sleeve and a few more ideas to share.[47] And, heck, you've come this far, so you might as well finish the race. Plus, it's a short book, so chill.

In the next chapters, I'll cover everything from mind control to weight loss.

Each chapter is outlined using the recommended structure of the 21-Day Miracle Process: Result, Emotion, and Plan. For the latter, I'll give you some ideas and guidelines; however, your 21-Day Miracle will be a plan of your choosing. Be creative. And have fun. Read this part of the book like you're in a cafeteria. Take a look at everything, then choose a few things. Like the Jell-O.

Downloadable PDFs of each plan are available for free on my website. You can see them all on one page at when you access the free training at www.EdRush.com/Bonus.

The 21-Day Mind Mastery Miracle

If you were to broadcast the average person's thoughts onto a movie screen, you'd conclude they were either crazy, convoluted, or criminal. I'm serious. Most people's thoughts roam from minute to minute. One moment they are filling boxes on a spreadsheet, the next moment they are dreaming of skiing in Vail. One moment they are focused on the meeting with the boss, the next moment they're thinking about the socks they left in the dryer.

Simply put: the average mind is a complete mess—a whirring, uncontrolled beehive of who-knows-what with thoughts full of whatever-happens-to-come-next.

Have you ever been in the middle of a perfectly good day off and then started getting nervous? One minute you're in the middle of a walk, enjoying the sunshine, and the next minute you're stressed about the big presentation next week, your finances, or your health.

The inability to control one's mind is the hallmark activity of a Hive-Minded Lemming. They don't control their mind. {48} Their mind controls them.

I have good news for you: you're not the "average person" and you're not a Hive-Minded Lemming anymore.

You do, however, have some work to do.

Imagine for a moment what it would be like to achieve total and complete control over your mind. What if everything you thought of was something you put there on purpose? Mind mastery is something you can accomplish. You just need a 21-Day Miracle to get you started.

Let's start with the 21-Day Miracle 3-Step Process we outlined in Part I.

First, state your desired result. Here is an example.

I have total mastery over my mind.

Then, associate a strong emotion to your desired result like this...

- I have total mastery over my mind.
- My thoughts are mine and I only dwell on the things I choose to dwell on.
- Stress and fear are gone. In their place are joy, happiness, and security.
- I use my mind to create amazing things in my life and business.
- I see many people coming to hear and listen to me because of my wisdom. (visual)
- My friends and family keep telling me how much I have changed. (auditory)
- I feel free for the first time in my life. (kinesthetic)

Finally, create the plan and take action.

Your plan for the 21-Day Mind Mastery Plan has two steps—and you can do them as quickly or slowly as you want. You can also overlap some of the steps—as you will soon see.

Step #1: Awareness and Observation

For one full week, all I want you to do is observe your thoughts. Just see what's happening up there. That's nearly impossible when you're in motion, so the best way to "observe" your thoughts is during brief periods of complete solitude and quiet.

Find a comfortable chair in a location where you won't be interrupted. Or go for a hike and sit on top of a mountain, under a tree, or next to a stream. If you're in a public place, grab some noise reduction headphones and drown out the world.{49}

If you want extra firepower, you might benefit from one of the many meditation apps on the market. They can be very effective for guiding your mind into a place of rest. The two apps I currently recommend are HeadSpace and BrainWave.{50}

HeadSpace can be found in the app store. It's a guided meditation tool and you get ten free days which is all you might need.

BrainWave can also be found in the app store and uses alternating sounds to get your brain into a more meditative state. It's just a few bucks and worth every penny.

Next, turn off all your media. Your phone has a real on / off function, so give it a shot. At the very least, switch it to airplane mode. Nothing bad is going to happen and you can obsess over your email again soon. Set a timer so you don't have to check the clock. Ten minutes should do the trick. Go for more if you want; just make it realistic. If you try for two hours on Day 1, you'll get frustrated and quit.

Now, close your eyes and, for about a minute, do nothing except focus on your breathing.

In. Out.

In. Out.
In. Out.

Now, step outside your head for a moment and just observe yourself with total and complete freedom and non-judgement. You're not trying to change anything just yet. All you're doing is getting a lay of the land.

What's happening up there?

Just take it all in. You're observing. So take some mental notes.

Are you thinking about work? Your family? Your body? Are you hot, cold, or comfortable? Are you daydreaming? Or are you thinking about this exercise and dang, how frustrating is this?

Take everything in. Don't worry about your thoughts, try to control them, or rein them in. Just watch.

And when the timer goes off, you're done. You don't have to do anything else. Your goal was to observe your mind—to be a passive, non-judgmental observer of your thoughts.

This might be the first time you've ever done this, so be kind to yourself. If all you do in ten minutes is catch one thought, just one short 4-second thought in ten full minutes of distraction, you accomplished the goal. In fact, observing the distraction *was* the goal, so you win either way.

The first step toward total Mind Mastery usually takes 7 days. There's no magic number of days and you can go shorter or longer if you want. You'll know you're ready to move on when you have a solid picture of how your mind works and what it takes to slow it down. And then it's time to move onto Step #2.

Step #2: Elimination and Replacement

Up until now, you've observed your thoughts as a passive / non-judgmental observer. You've seen thoughts and ideas float by and you were ok with that.

Now it's time to take action.

In this step, you're going to grab a hold of negative thought patterns and replace them with positive ones.

Here is a personal example. For most of my life, I have been fairly unhappy with my body. The first thing I would do most mornings was look at myself in the mirror and think, *Ugh. I don't like what I see.* Now, it doesn't take a psychiatrist to tell you that this kind of thinking ends up becoming a self-fulfilling prophesy. If you tell your body it's ugly, it will end up obeying that very command and you'll start looking like you sat on a radiator and ate yeast.

Then one day, as I was flipping through an old album, I caught a photo of me at age 17 without a shirt on. I was a chiseled rock of adolescent manhood. So disparate was the memory in my mind to the picture on the page that for a moment, I thought it was someone else.

And then it hit me, I hated my body back then too. I had spotted a negative thought and discovered that maybe I had been wrong this whole time.[51] The idea was liberating. So I decided to eliminate the negative thought pattern and replace it with a new one.

Instead of the *Ugh. I don't like what I see* thought and instead of reminding myself that *I need to lose 10 pounds,* I simply told myself how much I like what I see. That I was "fearfully and wonderfully made"[52] and that God gave me a gift in my body and I was glad to have it.

Here is the new belief I created, *I reject the lie that I am unhappy with my body. I choose instead to believe that I am fearfully and wonderfully made, that my body is a gift, and I love looking at what I see.*

At first nothing happened. Then slowly it began to take hold.

Next thing I knew, I grew to really like what I was seeing. The confidence was back and as an unexpected result, I started eating better and actually did lose some weight.

Was it magic?

Nope. It was a 21-Day Miracle.

I **observed** a negative thought. *Ugh. I don't like what I see.*

I **eliminated and replaced** it with *I am fearfully and wonderfully made, my body is a gift, and I love looking at what I see.*

I then put it into a **statement** that starts with *I reject the lie that* ____________ *(negative thought pattern)* and ends with *I choose instead to believe that* ____________ *(positive thought pattern).*

I reject the lie that I am unhappy with my body. I choose instead to believe that I am fearfully and wonderfully made, that my body is a gift, and I love looking at what I see.

The **result** was a whole new positive self-image and a body that began to obey my mind and actually start to look good.

Now it's your turn. Observe your thoughts. Eliminate the old patterns. Replace them with new ones. Put them into the *I reject the lie that* ____________ *(negative thought pattern) / I choose instead to believe that* ____________ *(positive thought pattern)* formula.

Saying it out loud helps. At first, you'll feel weird and the people next to you at Starbucks will think you're crazy. And then, like a change in the weather, the new thought pattern will take hold and you'll never know why you believed that old trash in the first place.

Your old thought patterns have been there for a while, so expect some resistance. This is a process and the 21-Day Mind Mastery Miracle is designed to give you the tools to quickly and easily overcome any negative thought pattern on demand.

The 21-Day Money Mastery Miracle

Compared to the small, single-engine biplanes that the U.S. military flew in World War I, today's combat fighters are sleek, stealthy, and capable of raining destruction upon the enemy at great ranges.

But while technology has changed a great deal over the past 80+ years, combat missions themselves really haven't changed that much at all. To put it simply, just about every mission can be summarized as follows:

1. Fight your way in.
2. Locate the **target**.
3. Destroy the **target**.
4. Fight your way home.

Fighter pilots *obsess* over targets. If you attend a briefing for a large-scale mission involving fighters, you will quickly discover that everything—and I mean *everything*—revolves around the target.

- Speed—something to get you to the *target* alive.
- Route—the way to the *target*.
- Intelligence—something you need to know about the *target*.
- Gas—something you need to make it to the *target*.
- Bombs—take them to the *target* and let 'em rip.

The U.S. military is so proficient because it understands that when you focus on one thing without any distractions, you accomplish your mission every time.

Which brings me to you. If you're like 99% of the people I have helped, money has probably been a problem. Sure, you've made some here and there. But looking back, you might not have much to show for it other than some spikes, some troughs, and a lot of frustration. If that's you, it may just be that you're focused on the wrong target.

But what if I told you there was a single secret that just about every wealthy person knows? And when implemented, this secret can unlock the kind of wealth you want with zero regrets and no strings attached?

Money mastery is something you can accomplish faster than you ever thought. You just need a 21-Day Money Mastery Miracle to get you started.

Let's start with the 21-Day Miracle 3-Step Process we outlined in Part I.

First, state your desired result. An example...

I have total mastery over money.

Then, associate a strong emotion to your desired result.

- I have total mastery over my money.
- Money flows quickly and easily to me from multiple sources.
- I see myself with total financial freedom. (visual)
- I hear people asking each other how I was able to do it so quickly. (auditory)

• I take a big breath and relax because I now have the resources help a lot of people. (kinesthetic)

Finally, create the plan and take action. Leverage heavily on what we covered in the last chapter. Money is all about how you think, so follow these steps again…

Step #1: Awareness and Observation
Step #2: Elimination and Replacement

To do that, we need to deal with some big, fat, ugly lies you've been told all your life.

Ok, fill in the blanks… "Money is the root of all ____________."

Money is the root of all **evil**, right?

Wrong. That's a total lie, it comes from the pit of hell, and smells like smoke.[{53}] First, whoever made this up thought he was quoting the Bible. He wasn't. He was decidedly MIS-quoting the Bible. The real verse goes like, “The **love** of money is a root **of all kinds of** evils.”{54}

Did you catch that? Somewhere along the line some Hive-Minded Lemming decided to cut a few words out of this very good verse, and in doing so, he completely changed the meaning. And drove millions into self-inflicted poverty. Turtle. Don’t listen to Turtles.

Now, here is the really sticky part of this lie.

If you thought someone was evil, what would you never do?
Answer: you’d never spend any time with them.

If someone thought you were evil, what would they never do?
Answer: they’d never spend any time with you.

“Hey Fred, what are you doing this weekend?”

"Aw, nothing—just going over to Joe's house. He hates me and thinks I am evil, so—you know—it should be fun," said no one ever.

If you've never had any "luck" with money and money doesn't seem to hang around you very long, the reason why might just be that you think it's evil. Seriously, money gets offended at that. He knows you think he's evil, so he'll just move along to someone who likes him—just like you would do.

One way to figure out what you think about money is to observe how you view wealthy people. Picture a very rich person—I'm talking private jet, Bentley, house in the Hamptons, and another one in Beverly Hills. The glass of wine he just spilled costs more than your best suit. His dog has more expensive jewelry than you do. His servants have servants.

What's the first thing that comes to mind? Honor? Respect?

For most people, the first response is jealousy covered over with a pious justification. They'll tell their friends how many people are homeless and how this rich person should be more unselfish. While secretly they simply hate the fact that someone has money—and they don't.

This little lie is so insidious that you see it everywhere in our Hive-Mind culture. Take movies. When is the last time you saw a movie that portrayed a wealthy person in a good light? How about never. Think about the movie *Titanic*. The rich people were on the top of the ship and they were boring, stuffy losers. The poor people were in the bottom of the ship, but boy did they have fun. The lesson of *Titanic*: if you want to be good and have a lot of fun, hang out below decks with a bunch of poor people.

I really can't think of one pop culture TV / movie example of an honorable rich person.[55] They're all jerks. Lex Luthor (*Superman*), Mr. Burns (*Simpsons*), Gordon "Greed is Good" Gekko (*Wall*

Street), and Scrooge McDuck are all evil —and very, very rich.{56}

Back here in the real world, the wealthiest people I know are making the biggest changes in the world for good. It's one thing to *want* to feed starving kids in Africa. It's another thing altogether to stoke a 7-million dollar check to actually feed starving kids in Africa.

So despite popular culture, if you keep looking at rich people with disdain, you'll never have any money. Remember, money only hangs out with people who like it. So be the kind of person money likes to be with.

Which brings me to my second point.

When I left the Marines back in 2006 and started my business, I realized something was wrong. I was working my tail off, but nothing was coming in. And any money I did make just went flying out of the window as soon as I made it.

It was at this precise moment that I realized there was something drastically wrong in my thinking. You see, Hive-Minded Lemmings only have two categories for wealth:

- Evil rich people
- Good poor people

Given those two options, any good-hearted, socially-conscious person would make the inevitable decision to forgo wealth in exchange for being "good."

I knew there was something wrong with this framework, so I decided to do some searching. I had to escape the Hive-Mind, and find a past culture that both had money and was generally regarded as noble. I eventually landed in Proverbs, a book written by a wise (and very rich) Jewish King around 950 B.C. I scoured the entire book from beginning to end, placing a small mark in my Bible next to every verse that had to do with wealth or poverty.

What I discovered simply blew me away. Instead of two categories, the wise wealthy King had four categories:

- Evil rich people.
- Evil poor people.
- Good rich people.
- Good poor people.

Now, given those four categories, the choice becomes quite clear. All other things being equal, I'll go ahead and choose to be a Good Rich Person.

That realization not only changed my mind, it also exploded my business. I quickly went from struggling to bringing in over a million dollars a year.[57]

And the biggest shift had to do only with focusing on the right target. Instead of trying only to be "good" and inevitably "poor," I chose instead to be both "good" and "rich." And like you, I am still a work in progress. I have had good years and bad years, boom and bust. But I have also been blessed to make a lot of money and help a lot of people too. All because of a single mindset shift: eliminating the "money is evil" lie and replacing it with "money is neither good nor evil; it is simply money, and I will choose to use it for good."

Which brings me to my next point.

Money is amoral—it is either good or bad depending on how you use it. Kind of like a gun. If someone uses a gun to rob a convenience store, that person is bad and the gun is being used for bad purposes. If a police officer uses a gun to apprehend the robber and save lives, that gun is being used for good purposes.

In other words, the thing itself is neither good nor evil. It's how you use it that determines its morality. So why not choose to be a good person who makes a lot of money and uses it to do good things?

Your 21-Day Money Mastery Miracle starts with nothing more than observation. Take a good hard look at how you think and feel about money and the people who have it. To do this, you may have to take a little field trip like I did last week. As a constant practitioner of what I teach, I decided to do a little experiment. So I drove up to the most expensive country club in San Diego. Listen, this place was nice. Perfectly manicured greens. Fairways that had grass on the grass. And a restaurant that would rock your world.

I walked into the clubhouse and looked around. And within seconds, I encountered a negative thought pattern in the form of jealousy. The 20-something golf-club members I came across could clearly afford the near-six-figure one-time entrance fee. Dang, that stung a bit. Listen, I am totally ok with rich old people. But rich young people—that opens a can of jealous worms inside me.

So I started making up a bunch of lies like *They probably inherited their money. They probably don't even work. Stuck up, lazy, good-for-nothing, trust-fund snobs.*

Two points. First, I am human. Second, even after years of work you still may find some old thought patterns that you need to replace. Just **observe** the lie and then **eliminate** the old thought pattern and **replace** it with something new using the same formula we used in the last chapter.

Observe a negative thought. *Money is the root of all evil.*

Eliminate and Replace it with *Money is neither good nor bad. So I choose to be a rich person who uses money to do good things.*

Then put it into a **statement** that starts with *I reject the lie that* ____________ *(negative thought pattern)* and ends with *I choose instead to believe that* ____________ *(positive thought pattern).*

I reject the lie that Money is the root of all evil. I choose instead to believe that Money is neither good nor bad. So I choose to be a rich person who uses money to do good things.

This is just an example, so be sure to do your own work in Step #1 to find your own negative thought patterns. Maybe your dad spent a lifetime telling you *Money doesn't grow on trees.* Maybe your mom told you a zillion times that *some people weren't meant to have money.* Whatever lie you have been told, eliminate and replace it. At first nothing will happen. Then, you'll start seeing some subtle shifts in your thought patterns. And finally (after about 21-Days), the lie will be gone and you'll be free to make as much as you want for the rest of your life. You might even end up joining that golf club with me.

It may be worth doing an entire 21-Day Money Mastery Miracle focusing on creating new, positive thought patterns about money.

The next step in your 21-Day Money Mastery Miracle is to create a plan for getting more money—a topic we will cover in more depth in The 21-Day Business Miracle. One way to stay in a

"Money Mastery Mindset" is a simple step that you can start doing right now.

The very first thing I do when I sit down in my office every day is check my bank account balance. Not email. Not text. Not social media. My bank account. You see, when I head to the office, I am purposefully leaving my family to create wealth and value in the world. It's an exchange that every entrepreneur around the world makes every day. But you can bet that if I'm going to leave my kids I'm going to have a good reason for it. My two reasons:

- To provide an income. (Wealth)
- To provide a service to my clients and customers that exceeds what they pay me. (Value)

Every great business focuses on these two things: wealth and value. And when you focus on these two, you'll soon find that not only do you benefit, but so does everyone else. Take this book as an example. Right now, I am in the morning of Day 3 of writing.[58] I am not with my family or my friends. I am not fishing or hunting. I am writing so I can create an income and provide a service. If you've read this far, I'm sure you agree that this book has exceeded the value over what you paid for it.{59} And, as for me, I get the side benefit of making some money with the message.

Win—win.

Plus, this book will have an intangible side benefit of bringing in more money as people buy my training products, attend my events, and perhaps become clients. {60}

Which brings me to my last point about making money. The fastest way to start making more of it right now is to focus on the things that bring the most value into the marketplace. I am not sure what that is for you, but I am guessing something just came to mind.

Whatever that is, start doing it. Now. And make sure you get compensated for the value you provide.

Your 21-Day Money Mastery Miracle starts with identifying and replacing old ways of thinking with new. And it continues with a 21-Day sprint doing activities that create income for you and value for the world.

The 21-Day Inner Warrior Miracle

> ***Disclaimer****: more than any other chapter in this book, this chapter sounds like it is written by a dude for dudes. On several occasions, I'll talk about being a man—and acting like a man. Hive-Minded Lemmings hate it when men talk about being men. That's because their idea of a "man" is a snowflake Instagramming himself in flannel.*
>
> *So if you're not a man, that's totally cool. I think you're great. Really. And if you're willing to be open-minded, you will get a lot of value in this chapter, especially when you apply it to your own life in your own way.*
>
> *Plus, some of the best "Inner Warriors" I know are women.*

Some time ago, I came to the shocking realization that I was losing my manhood. {61} Here I was, Mr. Fighter Pilot, the guy who literally wrote a book called *Warrior,* and I was losing my edge.

The transition came subtly. But slowly, I was becoming less wild and more *domesticated*.

Now listen, there is nothing wrong with home life. I love my family, conversations around dinner, and bedtime stories. I love Disneyland with my daughter dressed as a princess. I wouldn't give that up for the world.

But with all that came a subtle shift that I didn't catch until late in the game. You see, I was born a fighter. From early on, I loved a challenge and I was more than ready to face it head on. Football, baseball, and motorcycles. I could stare a man down and bring the heat. As a fighter pilot, I relished the thrill of the hunt, the stroke of victory, and the celebration of the win. In business, I would face problems head on. Close deals. Change destinies. And in life, I was eager to stand up for those who needed it most. To fight *for* the orphan, the destitute, and the homeless and fight *against* the pimp, the pusher, and the human trafficker.

But then—life happened.

I got busy and my focus started to blur. I wasn't doing anything wrong per se. I wasn't breaking any laws. I was just becoming *domesticated*. And it was slowly killing me.

It was in this exact moment that, with a shock, I realized I needed to make a change. Enter the 21-Day Inner Warrior Miracle. For 3 weeks, I would focus on being a man, acting like a man, and standing up for what I believed in like a man.

The results once again blew me away. I got my inner swagger back. I started tackling new challenges again. I started to think, feel, breathe, and fly.

And you can do this too.

Regaining the "Inner Warrior" is something you can accomplish faster than you ever thought. Like me, you just need a 21-Day Inner Warrior Miracle to get you started.

Let's start again with the 21-Day Miracle 3-Step Process we outlined in Part I.

First, state your desired result.

I am a warrior. I stand up for what's right and no one can stop me.

Then, associate a strong emotion to your desired result.

- I am a warrior. I stand up for what's right and no one can stop me.
- I am a man.[62]
- I think, act, and behave like a man. That means I use my strength to serve those who need it most and to create great value in the world.
- I see myself as a Gladiator, fighting to set people free. (visual)
- I hear the crowd roar and know they, too, believe in something greater. (auditory)

- I feel amazing because I am finally the man I was meant to be. (kinesthetic)

Finally, create the plan and take action.

The first step in the 21-Day Inner Warrior Miracle Plan plan is pretty much the easiest step in 21-Day Miracle history.

And the 2nd step is by far the hardest.

Yay.

Step #1—Purposeful Intake

I'll get right to the point and call this what it is—brainwashing. The good kind. Think about it this way. Your brain is dirty. It's caked over by years of hanging out with Hive-Minded Lemmings. It needs a good cleaning. If the term "brainwashing" brings up too many negative mental images, just go ahead and call it "BrainCleaning." Whatever you call it, together we're about to reprogram what's going on up there.

And we're going to start with what goes in *it*.

My rule: everything I allow into my brain is on purpose. My goal is to own every thought and control every minute. That spreads into all areas of life—from when I wake up to when I go to bed. The movies I watch, the books I read, the music I listen to, all—and I mean all—are digested with a purpose.

So the first thing I want you to do is resolve right now that what goes into your mind will be there because you put it there.

Movies

Let's start with movies. There is nothing like a good, well-written, well-produced movie to kindle the flame of the Inner Warrior. I can't explain it, but when you watch William Wallace win the Battle of Stirling, you start to feel that you can accomplish anything. You'll find yourself in your backyard, late at night, with a stick-as-sword in your hand screaming, "Sons of Scotland!"

It's probably the reason the people of old used to sit around the fire and tell stories of heroes. Not only was it entertainment, but it was also training. It was a reminder of a legacy to live up to.

So when I decided to regain the Inner Warrior, I went first on an "Ed Rush Man-Movie Fest."

Here is the list of what I watched during my sprint:

- *Braveheart*. Mel Gibson takes on the entire English army.
- *The Patriot*. Mel Gibson again takes on the entire English army.
- *Band of Brothers*. Lt Speirs…'nuff said.
- *Gladiator*. With the guy from A Perfect Mind. "A General who became a slave, a slave who became a

Gladiator, a Gladiator who defied an empire."

- *300*. Kind of like The Chippendales with swords.
- *Mandela: Long Walk to Freedom*. Great guy. Kind of had a crazy wife though.
- *The Matrix.* All 3 movies. "I know Kung fu."
- *Kingdom of Heaven*. Also known as "Infidels Have Feelings Too."
- *Spartacus*. 15 minutes of action jammed into 3 hours.
- *Cinderella Man*. Not Cinderella, Cinderella *Man*. Totally different.
- *Saving Private Ryan*. "Yes, Dad, you were totally a good man. Can you stop crying now?"
- *Fight Club*. One part *12 Monkeys* mixed with one part *The 6th Sense,* with a dash of *Rocky* (without gloves).
- *Das Boot*. I spelled that right. It's German so chill.

Here's the theme of every movie…

- The hero faces almost impossible odds.

- The hero wins.

Ironically, your theme is pretty much the same...

- You face almost impossible odds.
- You're going to win too.

After a month of watching that list of movies, you'll be ready to move mountains. Really. I know I was being a bit irreverent a minute ago, but it's probably to hide the fact that I cried through half of these movies. This stuff works.

Books

It's been said that poor people have big TVs and rich people have big libraries.[63] I paid attention when I first heard that and now I average reading one to two books a week. Everything being purposeful, here is a list of what I read to get back the Inner Warrior.

- *Call of the Wild.* Jack London. The story of a dog named Buck who finds his true self and becomes the dog he was meant to be. Sounds a lot like your story.

- *White Fang.* Jack London. Kind of the reverse story, but the dog is still the bomb.
- *To Build a Fire.* Jack London. Jack London was big for me back then. Spoiler—this one doesn't end well. Something about not being able *To Build a Fire*.
- Pierce Brown's *Red Rising Series.* This is your story—set on Mars. If you like sci-fi, read this now. If you don't like sci-fi, read this now.
- *King Solomon's Mines.* H. Rider Haggard. Just to remind you that real men existed before the Dollar Shave Club. Also, a really great name for a man who writes man-books—H...Rider...HAGGARD!
- *All the King's Men.* Robert Penn Warren. Prose like butter.

There is a more expanded "what I am reading list" with links on my website.[64]

Again, as with movies, each of these books was chosen with a specific purpose in mind. And, by the way, entertainment-for-the-purpose-of-entertainment is totally fine. If you want to read a book just so you can enjoy the book, go ahead and do that.

Just make it on purpose.

Music and Podcasts

We covered watching and reading, so let's move onto listening. Remember everything that goes into that brain of yours needs to be on purpose during your 21 Day Inner Warrior Miracle. That includes music, podcasts, radio, and everything else. Most people drive to and from work listening to whatever for no reason in particular. Most people are Hive-Minded Lemmings and you're not most people.

So if you mindlessly listen to music for no reason, that stops now. If you're listening to people droning on talk radio all day, chances are you'll end up angry or bitter. Again, entertainment or "I just like it" are fine. Just make sure you choose what you listen to and you have a good reason for it.

I put audio into two categories: music and words.

I choose music based on what I am trying to accomplish. Right now I am writing to jazz.[{65}] I also listen to classical music at work because I find it sets my mind in a solid "get things done" mode.

When I was on my quest to regain the Inner Warrior, it was all rock—and mostly hard rock like Rage Against the Machine, Alice in Chains, and Pearl Jam. That could put me at odds with some Christians who only listen to Christian music because they think anything else will make them do evil things. Some Christians are Hive-Minded Lemmings, so who cares. I put that music there for a reason.

Podcasts are a treasure trove for the lifelong learner. My only recommendation is to find a nice, even mix so you don't become too one-sided. For example, I like NPR's shows. But if all you ever listen to is NPR, you'll end up talking in whispers and thinking money grows on trees.

The same goes for shows on the other side of the aisle, or self-improvement podcasts. I like *The Tim Ferriss Show*, but I don't listen to every episode. First, I have other things to do. And second, when you only put one voice in your head, you end up all lopsided.{66}

The same goes for news. If you're going to listen, watch, or read the news, make sure it's on purpose. Every month or so, I personally go on a one week "news fast."{67} That way, I can clear my brain of any Hive-Mind thinking and get clear on what my real goals are.

Now, what I just shared with you is my list. It's not some prescription that you have to take two times a day. If you haven't figured this out yet, this book is a tool for you to implement in your own way and with your own timing. I am creating a movement, not a cult—the difference being you have your own mind, choices, and will. So go ahead and make your own list of movies, books, music, and audio learning.

And smile. This is going to be a lot of fun.

See, I told you that first step is super easy.

Now, to rain on your parade, your next task in 21-Days Inner Warrior Miracle is going to be way harder. In fact, you're probably not even going to do it. Actually, who knows, you read this far.[68] So maybe you'll crush this like you're crushing everything else.

Step #2—Take Purposeful Risks

Disclaimer time: I am a trained professional.[69] If you do what I do, don't expect the same results. You might even get hurt. Or get your feelings hurt.

And by all means, consult your doctor. She's[70] actually gone to school and she's way smarter than me. Plus, she has a stethoscope. I don't. When you ask her, she'll tell you not to do anything I recommend.[71] Listen to her. There's a solid chance that I am completely out of my mind.

Consider yourself warned.

Let's go back to the beginning when I said *you were made for more.*

You believed me and we're here together, one half of the way through this book talking about getting back your Inner Warrior.

We've come this far, why not go the rest of the way. Let's see what happens when you take the Red Pill, shall we?

What I am about to ask you to do will be simultaneously the simplest and most terrifying thing you will implement in this book. In short, I am going to recommend that you stand up for *something* or stand up for *someone*.

Now here is the rub. You can't do it as a group. And you can't do it in a crowd. In other words, joining 4,000 people at a March for Cow's Rights or whatever is great. It just won't train your Inner Warrior.

To do that, you have to be alone. Very, very alone.

For this task, you have to find someone (anyone) or something (anything) and stand up for them at least once in 21-Days.

Let me give you an example. A few months back, I was changing planes in Minneapolis, MN.[72] As I approached my next gate, the (very nice and very patient) lady at the counter made an announcement. "Hello, ladies and gentleman. I just talked to the captain and they're looking into a maintenance problem. No estimate as to when we'll be leaving. Right now, we're going to move our departure time one hour. Sorry for the inconvenience. We'll get you to San Diego as soon as we can."

I can tell you with 100% transparency that I don't get bothered by flight delays. It's not an issue for me at all. It is what it is and there's nothing I can do about it. So I just take it in stride. Part of that is because I've trained my brain to think that way. And part of it is I usually fly first class, which helps with the whole attitude thing. Flights really are much more enjoyable when you're not in a 10-round armrest bout with someone named Cletus.

Anyway, just as the (very nice and very patient) lady at the counter finished her announcement a (not very nice and not very patient) man yelled "Bulls*&t!"{73} at the top of his lungs and then walked over to the counter and showed the (very nice and very patient) lady both of his middle fingers.

Put on the gloves. Start the music. Here comes the warrior.

I sauntered[74] over to the (now very nervous looking) man, looked him in the eye and said the following, "Sir, I am a Marine. I fought for this country and saw my friends die. I didn't do all that to come home to see cowards like you do what you just did in front of all of us. What you did was wrong and it's high time someone told you so."

Nothing could have prepared me for what happened next. The (now very ashamed) man lowered his head and mumbled, "You're right. I'm sorry. I was having a bad day." And then he slinked away with his tail between his legs.

Then the (very nice and very patient) lady at the counter thanked me and offered me a drink voucher (valid for today)—which of course I didn't need since I was sitting in first class.

Drinks on me, First Class People! For I have bravely earned one of these here vouchers. Valid for today!

Let me tell you—that feels good. The standing up for someone part. Not the free drinks. Ok, that feels good too.

Here is another example. Again, this is from my life and your story is different. So just adjust the game plan to your life.

One of the things I do fairly consistently is ask random people if they would like prayer. I don't remember when I started this, but I do know it had something to do with me getting outside of myself and caring for people. At first, it was a pretty hard thing to do. Then I realized most people respond pretty well to that question and it became quite easy.

Here's how I do it. First, I ask, "Hi there. I am learning to pray for people and I was wondering if you had anything you want prayer for?"

At that point, they usually mention a health, money, or family issue.{75} Then I say, "Great, would you like me to pray for you right now?"

Then I just pray for them. It’s pretty easy. And you’d be surprised at how much people light up when they realize there’s someone in this cold, dark world who cares for them. Sometimes people get visibly moved and cry. Either way, they get prayed for—which helps. And I get a chance to stoke the fires of courage and train my Inner Warrior.

As for you and your next 21-Days, your brave rescue doesn't need to be so valiant.{76} But it does have to be done by you.

Now, I know what you’re thinking, *Ok, Ed, I get it. But what if I don’t find a situation where I can take a purposeful risk?*

Good question.

The answer is: You will.

I know it doesn’t make sense, but when you set out on your 21 Day Inner Warrior

Miracle, the world will conspire and present something to you.

And when it does, you'll know what to do.

The 21-Day Time Freedom Miracle

Speed is life.

That's a phrase I learned on Day 1 of fighter pilot training. The faster you fly the harder it is for the enemy to find you. And even if they do, 600 miles an hour of pure speed gives you a lot of power to break the tracking devices on most missiles.

Time is money.

Someone can take your car, your home, your savings, and your 401(k) and you can get it all back. But if someone takes just 1 minute of your time, just 1 minute, it's lost forever and you'll never see it again. Listen, we are all speeding at 60 minutes per hour to our ultimate end, so it's high time you got started changing the world.

To do that, you're going to have to take control over your time and your schedule. Enter the 21-Day Time Freedom Miracle to get you started.{77}

Let's proceed (now for the 4th time) with the 21-Day Miracle 3-Step Process we outlined in Part I.

First, state your desired result.

I am in charge of my time and my schedule.

Then, associate a strong emotion to your desired result.

- I am in charge of my time and my schedule.
- I have the perfect mix of work, leisure, and family time.
- I choose to only do the most profitable tasks.
- I see myself sitting outside at the end of a very productive day while I read a book and enjoy the sunshine. (visual)
- People keep telling me they can't believe how much I can get done in so little time. (auditory)
- I feel free for the first time in my life and I plan to keep it this way. (kinesthetic)

Then, create your plan.

To do this, you're going to need some tools. I get paid a lot of money to help high-performing CEOs and teams better manage time and deadlines. So I could go on forever on this topic. And maybe I will sometime. But not now. My goal in this chapter is to put a few tools in your hands that you can use during your 21-Day Time Freedom Miracle. The first of which is a damaging admission...

There is no such thing as time management.

I know that comes as a shock to you, especially after my saying I teach "time management." But it's true. You can't "manage" time. Time is going to move at the exact speed it always has and time really doesn't care what your plan is to slow it down.

So if time management doesn't exist, then what do successful people do to get more done in less time with less waste?

They manage what they can manage, namely: people, technology, and themselves.

People

One of the biggest mistakes I see leaders make is not empowering their people. Listen, if your team can't make a decision without *running a few things by you,* you don't have a team. They have you. If your business dies on the vine when you take a few days off, you don't have a business. It has you.

So make the decision right now that you're going to hire good people and empower them to make good decisions. I have a rule in my business that goes like this: if it's less than $500, go ahead and make the decision and tell me about it later. $500 is an important number for me and you'll discover why in just a minute.

While I am talking about people, you can go ahead and toss the idea of having an "open door policy." That breeds dependent people who don't think for themselves. I recommend a weekly, regular, scheduled meeting where they can ask all their questions. Have your meeting in a room with no chairs, tables, or food. You'll have a more efficient get together when your intern Rocco isn't popping Bruegger's Bagels in his mouth like he's a Pez Dispenser.

Technology

Remember, you're in charge. I check my email at certain strategic times a day and get real work done in the time in between. I am on social media an hour a week. Maybe. And that's usually to post content or sarcastically reply to someone. Never leave your email open all day. Never stay logged into Facebook. Both of those things suck time like Count Dracula.

By the way, I just cleared the 20,000 word mark in this book and I am still in Day 3. I did this by controlling media and focusing on the objective.

Yourself

What you do with your own availability is perhaps the single most important personal decision you will make. I personally "script" my work time—which I'll show you how to do in just a second. Whatever you do, just remember it's your time and you own it. Be your own boss. And, while I am thinking about it, make sure you schedule some Personal Development Time[78] so you can learn, grow, and think.

Speaking of time, there is a very simple way to figure out just what your time is worth.

Take an average workweek of 40 hours. Multiply it by the number of weeks in a year (round to 50).
That gives you a round 2,000 hours of "work time" per year.

Now, simply divide 2,000 into your income goal and you'll instantly discover what each hour is worth.

- If you want to make $100,000 a year, your time-value is $50 / hour.
- If you want to make $1,000,000 a year, your time-value is $500 / hour.
- If you want to make $10,000,000 a year, your time-value is $5,000 / hour.

So when you sit down to work on Monday morning at 9 a.m., you better make it a $500 hour. Otherwise you'll never get close to 7 figures.

Theoretically that also means you would be willing to part with up to $500 to free an hour of your time. Just remember that the next time you're tempted to hire that cheap, broke webmaster who lives in his parents' basement. He'll save you a few bucks and then eat up days of your time with shoddy work.

When it comes to the hours of your work day, I recommend scripting them out like a movie director.[79] Each day, for 21-Days, do the following:

1. First, make a list of the things you want to accomplish. (note—this "to do

list" is as far as most people go.)

2. Assign a priority to each task—from 1 to 10.
3. Assign a time to each task—from 10 minutes to 8 hours.
4. Then, script out the hours of your day starting with the highest priority tasks all the way to the lowest.
5. Start your first task and set a timer. {80} You're running against the clock. If you finish late, move faster next time. If you finish early, great. Take a break. Get coffee or check email.
6. Then start the clock again and get on to the next task.

Try it. You'll get more done in a single hour than most people do all day. And you'll get more done in a single day than most people do all week.

Your 21-Day Time Freedom Miracle starts with creating a plan for managing people, technology, and yourself. Then it continues as you create a value for every hour of your time and start scripting your work days. Do that now and, in 21-short-Days, you'll be a Time Master.

By now you probably figured out that I've barely scratched the surface when it comes to controlling and maximizing your time. I can only teach so much in a book that's designed to cover all the bases.

The good news is I have an entire course called "Fighter Pilot Productivity."

It's not cheap. But it is very good. And you're worth it.

You can find the link inside the Resource section at www.EdRush.com/Bonus.

Even if you don't take the course, you have enough to launch your 21-Day Time Freedom Miracle. Go forth and prosper. The world needs you and the clock is ticking.

The 21-Day Life Balance Miracle

Do you want to know how to achieve the Perfect Life Balance? Here is the 2-word answer…

You Can't.

That's because balance isn't a natural, normal, or even helpful state. Nature has two settings: sprint and rest.

So give yourself the freedom to give up the idea of balance.

It's not helping you. And striving for balance is getting in the way of the kind of joy, peace, and happiness you really want.

P.S. I know this chapter was a big tease, but I did it on purpose. It works better than just avoiding the topic altogether.

You're welcome.

The 21-Day Happiness Miracle

I wasn't particularly happy when I woke up this morning. I wasn't sad either. I was somewhere in between.

So I did a little experiment and put on Pharrell Williams's song "Happy."[{81}]

Four minutes later, here I am in front of my computer, hunting and pecking at this manuscript while my feet tap-tap-tap to this song playing on a loop.

And you want to know something? I am actually happy. Really happy. Dang, I feel good.

As we come to the little subject of happiness, the first lesson is: you've been told a lie that says happiness is caused by what's on the outside.

It's not. Happiness is 100% a function of what you choose. So, armed with this knowledge, and all things being equal, I'll just go ahead and choose to be happy.

Listen, I have been broke before. Actually, I was worse than broke—I was $143,000 upside down in debt that lasted for over a year. Except for a few stressed-out moments, I was pretty happy back then. Fast forward a few years and things are going well now and I'm pretty happy now too. Totally different circumstances; same emotion.

If you remember, a few chapters back I told you my rule of roller coasters: I don't ride them. And not riding a financial roller coaster means more peace, joy, and happiness.

So do you want to be happier? Great.

Let's start with the 21-Day Miracle 3-Step Process we outlined in Part I and create a 21-Day Happiness Miracle.

First, state your desired result.

I am happy and full of joy despite my circumstances.

Then, associate a strong emotion to your desired result.

- I am happy and full of joy despite my circumstances.
- I picture myself smiling a lot. (visual)
- People compliment me because I have a lot of fun doing what I do. (auditory)
- I feel great because I control my happiness and I control my emotions. (kinesthetic)

Then, create the plan and take action.

Because this chapter is about the way you think, I am going to lean heavily on the 21-Day Mind Mastery Miracle chapter. If you haven't read that chapter, go do that now and come back when you're done.

Happiness is an emotion, not a thought. But it is heavily influenced by your thoughts, so your first step in this 21-Day Miracle is to take mastery over what's going on in that brain of yours. The process is below.

Step #1: Awareness and Observation

Your first job is to just watch the silly little roller coaster of emotion go up and down based on seemingly nothing.

Watch as ideas flow and emotions move. Observe your brain getting super excited as the waiter comes around the corner with (what you thought was) your meal and watch as your brain gets all dejected when the waiter walks right by with someone else's tuna melt.{82}

Observe your emotions as traffic slows down and the guy in the right lane slowly becomes the jerk in front of you.

Again, just observe in a non-judgmental way and don't change anything (yet).

One clever little way to stay on top of this is to set a timer on your watch or phone so it automatically goes off every hour. The moment that alarm rings, ask yourself two questions:

- *How am I feeling right now?*
- *Why am I am feeling this way?*

Then grab a journal and write down your answers.

Step #2: Eliminate and Replace (With These "Back Door" Brain Hacks)

Once you have a solid grasp of your emotional roller coaster, it's time to take some action. In the 21-Day Mind Mastery Miracle chapter, I showed you how to eliminate and replace thoughts. Here we're going to eliminate and replace *emotions,* which means we're going to have to go a little deeper and come at this in a slightly different way.

Turns out your mind is just like a computer. It runs on a code and, under normal circumstances, you can just re-write some code to make a few changes. We did that together in the chapter on

Mind Mastery. The problem, however, with emotions is that they are a *response* to your way of thinking, not the actual thinking itself.

So we're going to have to make these changes using a coding "back door" called Your Body.

This is easier done than said, so humor me here. Right now, right where you are, try this.

1. Stand.
2. Hold your two fists in the air like Rocky Balboa did after he knocked out Clubber Lang—or like you would if your team just won the championship.
3. Smile as big as you can smile.
4. Scream "I Feel Amazing!" three times at the top of your lungs.

If you're reading this on a plane or in a public area, I get it. I was thinking about letting you wait until later, but no, just go ahead and do it right now. Stand there smiling like a champion screaming "I Feel Amazing." Do it. The exercise probably works better that way and you'll have the side benefit of challenging and strengthening your Inner Warrior.

Whether you do it in public or in private, you'll notice the moment you finish your third *I Feel Amazing* and put your hands down, two things will immediately and simultaneously happen:

1. You will chuckle.
2. You will actually feel **amazing**.

And that, my friends, is the power of the body to "back door" hack the brain.

I don't know why it works but it does. And **"I Feel Amazing!"** isn't the only hack. The number is limited only by your imagination.

For example, let's say you need some energy. Try a back door hack I call **"Rock Your Energy."** Just put on some heavy music like Led Zeppelin ("Stairway to Heaven" will do). Then really get into it and play air guitar around your room for ten minutes. If you prefer to be a vocalist, try the Rolling Stones and pretend you're Mick Jagger. I don't know why I thought of two artists from 50 years ago. So if you want something more modern, pick Katy Perry, Taylor Swift, or whomever. In less than ten minutes, you'll be full of good, useful energy and you'll take yourself less seriously.

Here's another one called **"The Gorilla."** Let's say your mind keeps coming back to a conversation you had last week and it's still bothering you. Stand and start banging your chest like a silverback gorilla while screaming, "My thoughts are mine." (Gorilla bang your chest) "And I am going to think what I want." (Gorilla bang) "As for that other thought—the one about the meeting—you're dismissed! Go away now!" (One final double-gorilla bang) Then grunt and eat a banana.{83}

Here is another hack that works wonders. I call this the **"Gratitude Hack."** For 21 straight days, do this one thing: spend just a few minutes of every day being thankful for something. It goes like this.

The very moment you wake up, in that very second, with your head still on your pillow and your dreams slowly fading away, speak out loud and say, "Thank you." And then start naming a few things…

- *Thank you for a good night's sleep.*
- *Thank you for my healthy body.*
- *Thank you for the meals I had yesterday.*
- *Thank you for my family.*
- *Thank you for Ed Rush for he is both handsome and wise.*[84]
- *Thank for the opportunities I have before me today.*

I did this little exercise a year ago and it still sticks. I knew it was really working when, in the dream I had just before I woke up, I was saying "Thank you."

Another hack is one I call **"The Present-Minded Meal."** For 21-Days, your only job is to be 100% present during meals. It works like this:

1. Take a bite of food.

2. Put your fork down and rest your hands.
3. Now focus 100% of your attention to what's going on in your mouth.
    - Chew slowly.
    - Taste every bite.
    - Notice the differences in texture and taste.
    - Focus.
4. When you're completely done with that bite, pick up your fork or sandwich and do it again.
5. Repeat until you are full.

This works so well because the exercise spreads into other areas of your life. The opposite emotions of happiness and joy are fear and anxiety. If you are the kind of person who spends a lot of time thinking about the past, you'll dwell on fear. If you're the kind of person who obsesses over the future, you'll tend to be anxious.

But, if you are the kind of person who can simply focus on the present, you'll experience neither fear nor anxiety.

You'll be happy.

During your 21-Day Happiness Miracle take a very close look at your language patterns as these tend to control thoughts and emotions. For example, Hive-Minded Lemmings use phrases like, "That person made me really angry." The problem with this kind of thinking is that no one can make you *feel* anything. Every emotion is a choice. And you are in control of your choices. So the next time some bozo cuts you off in traffic and you start honking your horn like a Manhattan cabbie, just whisper to yourself, "I chose to be angry at that person." Three times of doing that and your traffic rage will dissipate and you'll smile in the middle of the road-going-nowhere knowing you can do almost anything.

In the beginning of your quest for emotional mastery, you're going to have to use these "back door" hacks more than once. For example, maybe you feel a bit down, but you counter that with a good strong **Gorilla**. Five minutes later, you might start to feel those old emotions coming back. **Gorilla** again. An hour later, they might come back (only this time you'll notice they're not as strong). **Gorilla** again.

In other words, **Gorilla** until the emotion turns and walks out of your life in shame. Which would be totally ironic if the emotion *was* shame.

So, whatever "hack" you choose during your 21-Day Happiness Miracle, just be sure to take a full 21-Days to observe your emotions and replace them with emotions that serve you and your purpose. The world is a tough place and it's even tougher if you're cranky all the time.

You happy now?

The 21-Day Body Miracle

There's an insidious little lie that, given enough time, will wreck our culture. We've convinced ourselves that, because of science and innovation, we are so much smarter and better than everyone who came before us. And in the process, we've made the dual mistake of being both wrong and arrogant.

Let me give you an example. For the last 5,950 years of recorded human civilization, people didn't "work out." It wasn't even an actual phrase until 100 years ago. If you took a time machine back 250 years and told someone you were going to "work out," they would have assumed that you were literally going to "work"..."out!"

Enter the 1900s. Society moved from fields and factories to little Dilbert-sized cubicles and we lost the kind of work that kept our bodies in shape. Then along came McDonald's and the rest was history. We encapsulated ourselves in little speed bubbles called cars, made even more convenient for drive-through windows because heaven knows we wouldn't want to actually have to *walk* four yards across a parking lot.

Now, shed the Hive-Mind and think with an independent brain. With obesity and heart disease at an all-time high, could it be possible that *we* are the ones who are wrong? Is there a chance (no matter how slight) that with all the scientific advancements and innovation, we actually have it wrong and they actually had it right? Is it possible that the single most enlightened culture in history may be dead-in-the-water wrong on quite a lot of things (and we have only ourselves to blame)?

That's exactly what I am saying—that maybe we aren't so super smart after all. Our ignorance is so deep you can see it on every social media outlet.

It's kind of important too. Because, as we tackle the concept of fitness, you need to know that I am going after it like someone from the 1700s, not someone from today.

So don't send me letters with quotes from scientists as to how right we are here in the present day.

Now onto the fun part: you actually can have the body you want. In fact, in just a few weeks you could be on track to looking and feeling great. You just need a…(drum roll) 21-Day Body Miracle to get you there.[85]

We'll use the simple 21-Day Miracle 3-Step Process that I outlined in Part I.

First, state your desired result.

I look great. I am at my ideal level of fitness and I eat healthy food that I love.

Then, associate a strong emotion to your desired result.

- I look great. I am at my ideal level of fitness and I eat healthy food that I love.
- I have renewed mastery over food. I love what I eat—it's good, healthy, and fresh.

- I follow a movement routine that makes me feel amazing.
- I look at myself in the mirror, and hey, I look great. (visual)
- I scream, "I feel great!" at the top of my lungs. I don't care who hears. (auditory)
- I feel confident in how I look and feel. (kinesthetic)

Finally, create the plan and take action.

I am going to break down your 21-Day plan into 2 categories: food and movement. I'm using the word "food" instead of "diet." There's too much baggage attached to that word diet and it tends to conjure up thoughts of food trays, meal plans, and late-night infomercials. I'll use the word "movement" instead of "Exercise" for the same reason. You'll see why in a few pages.

Food

Food is absolutely the most vital aspect to having a great body, so let's start there and grab some low-hanging fruit first with a very important starting point.

Don't drink your calories.[86]

Most people's diets are dead-in-the-water because they chug 32 oz. of refined sugar every day. The bottle says "diet," but the bottle was created by a Hive-Minded Lemming. The bottle lies. There's nothing diet about it.

So, if soda or any other kind of sugary drink is an issue, you might just want to launch a single 21-Day Body Miracle doing nothing more than not drinking whatever you are currently drinking.

I personally only drink one of 3 things: water, sparkling water, and black coffee. I never even think about soda.

Which brings me to a clever little secret when it comes to diet: it's all in your mind. I mean that. Have you ever wondered why some people smoke, drink, or gorge and some people don't? It's a brain thing. What that means is, in just a few days of executing your new habit, your body will adjust. The rest is upstairs in that grey matter of yours. So if you skipped ahead, it's worth going back and reading the 21-Day Mind Mastery Miracle chapter.

Another 21-Day Body Miracle you might want to try is 3 weeks only eating food that is 100% organic, gluten-free, dairy-free, and sugar-free. That's it. And it's easy once you get started because there are about a billion menu options. You can eat as much as you want and whenever you want.

One of the reasons this focused meal plan works so well is that it requires you to actually think about everything you eat. And the thinking part is enough to train your brain that what you eat is important.

If you go this route, here is a general idea of what to expect. For the first few days, as your body adjusts, you'll feel horrible and your brain will scream for the old slop. After a week or so, your energy will increase and you'll start to feel really good. After 21-Days, you will have a renewed sense of what is healthy for you and your body will look a lot better.

Then, on Day 22, I want you to eat whatever the heck you want. Go to Wendy's and Cinnabon in the same meal. Chug a liter of Diet Coke while standing in the aisle of the 7-11. Pour yellow imitation cheese over Cheetos. Pound another energy drink. Dump salad dressing on your fries.

Gorge yourself. Have a blast. Really go for it.

And that night, as you lie in bed feeling horrible, you'll realize over the previous 21-Days, you created a new healthy habit and you will smile. You'll discover that your body actually likes good, fresh food. You'll know that the obsession over the old junk was all in your head. And you'll never eat the same way again.{87}

Penn Jillette (from Penn & Teller) lost 100 lbs. by eating nothing but potatoes.{88} He doesn't know it, but he's a 21-Day Body Miracle graduate. He discovered that you can, in fact, do anything, as long as you're willing to just get on with it and do it.

Movement

Here's a damaging admission: I really hate working out. I think it's a boring waste of calendar space. I have a very limited amount of time and I want to change the world. That means I don't want to spend 1 hour a day (every single day) running in circles, pedaling a bike that goes nowhere, or kicking aimlessly at the air.

I think it's all silly and senseless. And the fact that so many people spend so much time thinking about nothing but working out should tell you something about the narcissism that pervades the Hive-Mind.

Go back 250 years in that time machine, only this time bring someone back with you. It can be anyone, but you might as well be creative. Pick Thomas Jefferson since he is both wiry and strong. As soon as you land in the present day, bring T.J. to the local gym and watch him laugh hysterically. Uncontrollably. Do you know how ridiculous we look to someone from the 1700s? Prior to 1950, people lifted things only because they needed lifting.

So where is she going? T.J. asks with a smirk as he watches a chiseled behemoth of a woman run a thousand miles an hour on a treadmill.

Nowhere, T.J., she's—oh—nevermind.

Sigh.

That said, I do think keeping your body in functional shape is both important and necessary. What I just said is not be used as an excuse to sit on the couch and eat potato chips while cracking jokes with an imaginary Thomas Jefferson.

But if you exercise, make it something functional. Make it something life-realistic that gets your mind off the stress. In other words, not an exercise bike or an elliptical or a stair climber. Hive-Minded Lemmings ride or run on things that stand still. It looks ridiculous because it *is* ridiculous.

Don't be ridiculous. Be you.

The list of functional things you can do to stay in shape is quite endless, but here are a few ideas:

- **Biking**—in other words, ride an actual bike on actual trails or roads. The kind of riding where you see actual things go by. The kind of riding that you can do without a TV. I like mountain biking, but I also like riding on roads. So I had my mountain bike fitted with "cyclocross" tires so I can do both. Side note: I listen to purposeful music or podcasts while I ride. (See the chapter called The 21-Day Inner Warrior Miracle for more on that).

- **Basketball, Baseball, Softball, or anything else that ends with the word "ball."** Playing a good game of basketball down at the gym will give you the best cardio you've had in weeks and you won't even notice it.

If you are horrible at ball sports, go anyway. Just having the courage to get on that court will actually help your self-esteem and cure the memory of being picked last in 6th grade.

• **Boxing. Wrestling. Jiu Jitsu.** {89} There is nothing like getting punched in the face or "choked out" to make your spirit really come alive. And don't worry, if you go someplace where they teach these arts for a living, you'll be in a safe, fun environment with a lot of beginners to punch.

• **Running. Walking.** Real running on real ground. If I run (which is basically never), I run on trails.

• **Hiking.** I am a big fan of hiking. Not only is it great exercise, but you connect with nature and escape the Hive-Mind. You also have a (slight) chance of being eaten by something, which works wonders for your Inner Warrior.

- **Yard Work / Manual Labor.** Look around. Chances are your house needs a little work. If not yours, maybe you know someone in your family or a charity that needs something done. Why not kill two birds with one stone and get a workout with your work?

- **Functional Weight Lifting.** I like lifting weights that aren't connected to a machine or a wall. Squats are probably the single exercise that covers the bases. Kettlebells look ridiculous, but work wonders on your back (and butt).

- **Yoga. Stretching.** I do this maybe once a year so I'm no expert. All I know is every time I do yoga or stretch, I tell myself *I should do this more often.* There's a great app called "Yoga Studio" you can use if you're interested.

Again, this is just a short list. Use your imagination and be creative. You might find you get in great shape and have a lot of fun in the process.

What I just gave you under food and movement is less of a step-by-step prescription and more of a smorgasbord. {90} Go ahead and use that independent brain of yours and create a plan that works for you. On a 21-Day Body Miracle, I don't work out every day—usually every other day. So be sure to make your plan realistic enough that you can walk up the stairs when you are done.

One last thing about food and movement: don't weigh yourself.

If you really need to, just do it every month or so. My experience with scales is that they hurt more than they help. My recommendation is to focus more on the activity than the result. Success in food and movement is found in both creating and following a plan.

When you do that, you'll start looking and feeling great. And as a side benefit, you'll get more done and help a lot more people.

Hey look, it's Thomas Jefferson on a StairMaster.

The 21-Day Relationship Miracle

Somewhere back in the introduction to Part II of this book, I said the following words, "Some topics I am better on than others and you'll quickly figure out which is which by chapter length."{91}

Between us, I had this very chapter in mind when I wrote those words. Let's just say I'm not exactly a "relationship expert." Nor am I a "people person." I prefer to be by myself—like I am right now—with some music and a word document. So let me be very direct; you really shouldn't take relationship advice from me. It will probably end badly and it will be mostly my fault. You should probably just go ahead and skip this and get relationship advice from someone who smiles a lot and loves everyone.

That said, I have a few pieces of relationship advice that can not only turn you into an amazing, likeable, gregarious person, but will also have the side benefit of setting your bad relationships right again. Chances are you haven't heard this strategy before, so you might find something here that works for you.

Much like anything, there are two ways to get things done: the long way and the short way. The long way takes years of counseling and often ends in frustration, pain, and loss. The short way is called the 21-Day Miracle and has the power to change anything in 3 short weeks.

So if you want to radically change your relationships, a 21-Day Relationship Miracle might just do the trick.

As usual, let's start with the desired result:

I have uplifting relationships filled with love and empathy, and I am protected by proper boundaries.

Then, attach some emotion to your outcome:

- I have uplifting relationships filled with love and empathy, and I am protected by proper boundaries.
- I only spend time with people who are a blessing to me.
- I only spend time with people I bless.
- I picture all my family members enjoying time with me. (visual)
- They keep telling me how thankful they are that we are together. (auditory)
- I feel so connected and fulfilled. (kinesthetic)

Once that's done, it's time to create a plan.

Your plan has three steps—the second one being the hardest. Like a good grape farmer, you're going to do three things to make your relationships flourish and bear fruit: first, you will take a good hard look and assess the vine, next you will prune it, then you will help it grow.

Step #1: Evaluate Your Relationships

Here is a 1-hour exercise that you can do on Day 1 of your 21-Day Relationship Miracle: open the contacts section of your phone and make a list of everyone with whom you have a relationship. Mom and Dad count, as do your siblings and any friends or business associates. The guy who cleans your pool doesn't count, unless you happen to be close, and then we have other things to talk about.

Having made your list, I want you to give each person a score.

> **1**—This person makes your life harder, is difficult to be around, or steals energy from you. In other words, they are a gigantic pain in the posterior.
> **2**—This person neither adds nor takes away from you. Neutral.
> **3**—This person gives you more life and you love being around them.

Be as mercenary and emotionless as you can when scoring your list. Be a robot. If you can't, get someone else to help you (preferably someone who isn't a 1). Don't bump anyone up just because they are close or family. If your sister is a horrible person and she makes your life hell, she is a 1.

Now that you have your list, let's move onto Step #2 and what to do with all those 1s.

Step #2: Prune Negative Relationships

Prune might be the wrong word. Perhaps we should try something more aggressive like: hack, chop, annihilate, or destroy.

Sound awful? It is.

That's because there is a long list of people in your life right now who you just scored 1 that shouldn't be there at all. Call them what you want, they are sucking away your time, energy, and ambition. I don't know how they got into your life. Maybe you met at college. Maybe they live next door. Maybe they are married to your spouse's best friend. {92} Maybe they gave birth to you.

However they got in your life, it's time to do one of two things: either **Eliminate Them** or **RTR Them.**

Eliminate Them is for people you have a choice about being around (i.e. not family). Also, **Eliminate Them** doesn't involve the mob. I may be an introvert, but I'm not that cold.

All I am saying is just never talk to them again.

Ever.

Sounds hard, but it's really easy. If they ask, just say you're busy. If they text, don't text back. If they call, don't answer. They'll get the point soon and you'll be free.

I know you just told yourself nine reasons why you can't do this. And I know you probably think I am the meanest person on Planet Earth. Just go back a page.

You just scored this person a 1, for crying out loud. That means they are awful and need to go. You don't owe them anything, so just get on with it.

RTR means "Re-Define the Relationship." This is for people who are 1s, but you have no choice about being around them. The list includes: co-workers, your boss, or close family members. For these folks, you're going to have to have a conversation. I know this idea scares the dickens out of you and that's ok. You'll soon find that there is a lot of power on the other side of this little discussion and wish you had it a long time ago.

The process is simple, just sit down with the person and say something like:

Hey there, (insert name of time-sucking, evil-person-who-scored-a-1), we need to talk so have a seat. I don't know how you are going to take this and frankly I don't care, but I've come to the realization lately that you're not a very positive person to have in my life. I want to be around you, but here are a few examples of things I could do without. (Insert a few examples). So, as a way of honoring our relationship I thought it was important to bring it to you so we could talk about making this better.

Pause.
Listen.
Say whatever comes to mind.
Don't back down.
And then (just like that) you're done.

After saying what you have to say, you're going to get one of only two responses. 99% of people you confront will immediately begin to apologize and make things right. Well done.

The other 1% will stiffen their necks and fight back.

Either way, you've taken control and **Redefined the (wobbly) Relationship,** so you win.

By the way, I know you're going to be super nervous going into that conversation and that's fine and normal. Just press through it because you have two choices: a hard 20 minutes or a hard 20 years. Plus, it's not your fault the person is a 1. It's theirs. So stop making excuses for them and bending your life around their dysfunction.

Don't spend 4 days practicing the conversation in your head or writing it all out either. Just do it. Speak from the heart. And that means speaking in person if you can. Otherwise on the phone. Never use email, a letter, or text messaging for this conversation. Never. Most people say things over email that they would never say in public, so if you want to get a good, healthy, honest response from the 1, speak to them person-to-person. Plus, you'll resolve this quicker that way, in 20 minutes instead of an email battle that turns into a consuming "reply to all" slugfest.{93}

You can do this.

Oh—and one more reason to have this conversation now: you'll get a big reward at the end.

Within minutes of the conversation ending, you will feel actual power surging into your body. Know what that is? It's all the strength you've been giving that person all these years. That power is all coming back to you—and it feels good.

Nature abhors a vacuum, so when you cut ties with your horrible 1-rated excuses for "friends" the world will conspire to give you new ones. Only this time, they'll be the kind of people you want to be around. They'll encourage and inspire you. And you'll be glad you took the time and had the courage to set things right.

Step #3: Grow Your Good Relationships

So we dealt with the 1s. And it was hard, but you did it. Now you feel good—really good. So let's take care of the other two categories.

Nothing happens with 2s. They are just there. And after that last page, I am sure you're happy to hear that.

Now that you've freed up some space and don't have all those abhorrent and abominable 1s in your life, it's time to dedicate some attention to the fascinating and fabulous 3s.

Here is a fun little 21-Day Relationship Miracle exercise that you can do right now.

For a full three weeks, spend just 10 minutes a day doing nothing more than *thinking* about someone you love. You don't even have to do anything for them. Just find a comfortable, quiet place, start your timer, and imagine what it's like to be them. Do that. Close your eyes and imagine that you are, in fact, them.

- What were they thinking about when they went to bed last night?
- What did they feel like when they woke up this morning?
- What are they thinking about now?

- What's a big priority for them this month?
- If they could go anywhere on a vacation right now, where would it be?
- What books are they reading?
- What movies have they been waiting to watch?
- What's the biggest challenge they are having in life?[94]

The list of possible questions is endless. The point is simply to be them—if only for 10 minutes a day. The trick to this little exercise can be summarized in the word empathy. And even though I told you that you don't need to do anything, you'll soon find over the course of 3 weeks, you will start doing things for them. A lot of things.

As for that 3 you thought about for 10-minutes a day—they'll start looking at you in a totally different light. They'll see a kindness that they never thought existed and a new awareness in your eyes that will begin to mold, shape, and change everything for the better.

And after coming all that way, you will discover that great relationships aren't about you after all. That's why the "pruning" process was so important. It felt downright selfish but now you realize the person who really paid the price was the person you just did this exercise about.

So get on with it then. Make your list, start pruning, and get growing. You might just find that love really is the answer after all.[95]

The 21-Day Business Miracle

Want to know what's going to change the world? It's not government, legislation, media, church, or charity.

It's business.

I know that sounds shocking, especially since our Hive-Mind culture loves to vilify the whole money-making thing. They sit comfortably at the local coffee house and wax eloquently about the evils of business while sipping a frothy mocha provided by a *business* who bought coffee beans from another *business* who paid yet another *business* to farm the beans and still another *business* to fly them there.

They go Twittering about how evil *business* is while riding in their happy little cars (invented and built by a *business*) that is fueled by gas from yet another *business* while listening to pop music on an iPhone created by still another *business*.

Their ignorance is breathtaking.

Want proof that business is the most noble profession on Planet Earth?

Try this little thought experiment. Imagine there is a giant spaceship orbiting the globe that swoops up every pastor, counselor, nonprofit employee, politician, and social worker.[96] The ship then orbits Earth with nothing to do but watch for a full week.

Know what happens?

Nothing.

Sure there are a few small disputes, some marriages need help, and some sermons get skipped. But by and large the spaceship lands a week later to a world that's pretty much the same.

Now try the same experiment. But in this case, swoop up every business owner, entrepreneur, and salesperson. You don't even need a week to see the results. Within about 4 hours, world economies will completely collapse. Cars will stop running. Phones won't work. Pandemonium. Looting and riots. The spaceship touches down 7 days later to a planet that has completely destroyed itself. And all those folks that used to work in HR and complain about why they were getting paid less than the sales team? They're in a bunker huddled up shivering and whimpering in burlap.

That, my friends, demonstrates the noble importance of business.

So smile. The world hasn't collapsed and that's because of you. A good business does two things really well: it makes money and it provides a service of a value greater than what it receives in return. And your job, whether you own a business or not, is to make sure that happens.

Now, it's easy to get sidetracked and lose focus, especially when you have a world to take care of. Most business owners get way less done and make far less than they should. So if you want to grow a business, explode a brand, and change the world, there's nothing quite like a 21-Day Business Miracle to accomplish some specific strategic objectives.

Let's start with the 21-Day Miracle 3-Step Process we outlined in Part I.

First, state your desired result. In this case, make it something big enough to make a difference, but small enough that you can get it done. I'll use this current book project as an example...

I have written a book, created a website, and launched a training product called the 21-Day Miracle.

Then, associate a strong emotion to your desired result.

- In 3 short weeks, I have written a book, created a website, and launched a training product called the 21-Day Miracle.
- The wisdom I share will help millions of people change their lives and the world.

- I picture the people helped by this message and I smile. (visual)
- People keep telling me how much they've learned and grown through the 21-Day Miracle. (auditory)
- I feel amazing because I created great value in my business and helped so many people. (kinesthetic)

Finally, it's time to create the plan and take action. Create an achievable but big enough plan to get done what you want to get done. Include team members.{97}

Then set in place the one thing that will ensure you get it all done: A deadline. Listen, without a deadline, you don't have a plan. Without a deadline, nothing is going to happen. Most people, myself included, are giant procrastinators. That means if you're going to get something accomplished, you need to hold your feet to the fire and make it happen.

For this little project of mine, my first deadline was the book. I gave myself 4 days to write the manuscript—a giant impossible leap (until I did it). I am just past the halfway mark of Day 4, I've written over 25,000 words and I'm feeling good about being done by the end of today.

Today is Thursday. My next deadline is Monday. By then, I'll have completed two editing passes and sent this on to my real editors.

For the next two weeks, I'll knock out the cover, layout, and launch the book both on Kindle and paperback. I've got enough of an online following to make it a #1 best seller on launch day.

While that is happening, I'll create the website in a couple of days and launch the training product (3 days). And in 21-short days, I'll be done and kicking back to celebrate a completed project that's going to change the world.

Here's the point: if I hadn't given myself a set of deadlines, I would barely have an outline by now.

Not everyone is going to write a book or complete a project like mine, so I thought I would share a few more ideas on how to grow your business and brand. I do this for a living, so I could go on forever. I don't have forever, so I'll limit myself to some basic principles that apply to most brands. These are big picture strategies so pick what works for you and build a 21-Day Business Miracle around 1 or 2 of these ideas. And if you need help, get it. There are people like me that specialize in helping you turn strategy into implementation, so hire someone to help you speed up the process.[98]

This will work no matter your size, number of employees, or unopened emails. It's a simple way to look at your complex problem that can give you more revenue with (way) more peace of mind.

Ok, let's get started. Every business (and I mean every business) needs these three things...

Step #1—Positioning / Authority.

Let's face it. The marketplace has gotten more crowded and more complicated. Ten years ago, you could get new customers with cheap ads on Google or with easy referrals. Now, Google's prices block out most businesses and Facebook ROI's[{99}] float around 1:1. Not to mention the fact that your once-empty niche now has 4 times more competitors (who mostly all compete on price).

Add to that the increased skepticism, increased difficulty in finding quality team members, and our anti-business / government-control / excessive-taxation atmosphere and you'll probably come to the conclusion that now is not a good time for growth and an even worse time if you're starting up.

But what if you could stack the deck (legally) in your favor? What if you could create an advantage in the marketplace that no one could (or would) follow?

You do that by creating your own positioning or authority in the marketplace. In other words, you create something that sets you apart—that makes people choose you no matter the price—something that makes them brag about the fact that they *get to work with you*.

Easier done than said.

That's because the interwebs have given you everything you need at your fingertips. You just need to—do it. The key with positioning is this—your prospect should soon see you as an expert, not as a salesperson.

Here are a few ideas on how to create your own "positioning / authority."

Write a Book

Most people think it takes three years and a cabin in the woods to write a book. Try three weeks. You don't even need the woods. A book is basically a word document with a cover. You've probably written enough emails this week for a book.

Listen, if I sat down with you for a few hours and just asked you questions about your business, you'd speak enough content for a good book. Just record the answers, transcribe them, have a good edit, and you're done.

Launch an interview show or podcast

Think about it—what would it mean to your brand if you interviewed all the movers and shakers in your niche? Answer: a lot. "A rising tide lifts all boats" and connecting with connected people means more umph for your brand.

Gear required: nothing more than a mic and recorder. Below in the footnotes are the ones I use.{100}

Speak

There's a solid chance your industry has some kind of trade show once a year. Most have several. It's one thing to pay for a vendor booth and shove candy and cards in people's faces.

It's quite another thing to be a speaker.
Speaker = Expert.
Expert = Authority.
Authority = "I want to do business with them."

Wait, Ed, how do I get a speaking slot?

Just ask your association. Most have a page on their website that says "Call for Speakers." They need you. So get out there and hustle. Make a couple of calls.

I don't know what I would speak about?

Yes, you do. Stop making excuses. Just get up there and tell them something like...

- The 5 Biggest Mistakes (insert industry) Make When Trying to Get (insert some challenge they have here)

- E.g. **The 5 Biggest Mistakes CRM Companies Make When Trying to Get New Customers**

- 3 Ways to (insert some challenge they have here)
    - E.g. **3 Ways to Decrease Customer Support Problems**
- 7 Myths You've Been Led to Believe About (insert some niche-specific issue they have here) And How to Break Through All 7 to (insert something they want)
    - E.g. **7 Myths You've Been Led to Believe About the Franchise Process and How to Break Through All 7 to Get More Franchisees Now**

I could do this in my sleep.

I know you might get all nervous when you speak. Do it anyway. First, no one will notice[101] and second, it will excite your Inner Warrior to be up on stage.

Anyway, those are just three of many positioning / authority tools. Others include writing (blogs, LinkedIn Publisher articles, Facebook posts, articles in trade journals or news outlets), doing media interviews, creating videos for a YouTube channel or your website, and more.

Step #2—Get and Close Deals or Customers

It's shocking how much of an owner's time can be spent on things that don't drive revenue. People, technology, meetings, email, distractions, planning, and more meetings.

Great businesses focus on two things:

- Activities that drive revenue.
- Activities that drive a great customer experience.

That's it. So no matter what you do, take a good look at how you allocate your time. Most of the business owners that come to me as clients say they are spending less than 10% of their work hours driving sales. By the time I'm done with them, it's more like 80%.

Plus, most of your problems can be solved with money.

Don't believe me? Ok, think of your biggest problem right now. Tech, people, infrastructure? Now imagine I just gave you a check for 2 million dollars. How many of those problems can be solved right now? How about all of them.

Here is a fast track 21-Day Business Miracle you can do right now. Commit to spending one full hour every day for 21-Days doing nothing more than getting clients or customers. Just start the clock, close all media, and work. Make the sales calls you need to make. Create a new offer. Build a sales funnel.

When you do this for 21-Days, three things will happen. First, you'll actually make a bunch more money. Second, you'll be blown away by how much time you haven't been spending on money-making activities. Third, you will create a new habit.

Step #3—Build the Team and Infrastructure to Support Steps #1 and #2.

In my experience, most founders start at #3 (which is precisely the wrong place to start).

The first thing to do is create authority. You can do this as a one-person gang (with maybe one or two outsourced people to edit, create graphics, or run a camera).

The second thing is to drive sales. You do this by creating a compelling offer that solves problems and keeps people awake thinking about it.

Then (and only then) you build you team. Third.

If you read any of the business magazines on the market today you've probably been sold a gigantic lie. You see, it's common for these magazines to interview some successful entrepreneur who just sold his company for 7 gabillion dollars to Facebook. During the interview, the now very successful, wealthy (yet totally bored) entrepreneur engages in a little revisionist history. He is asked by the (also now totally bored) interviewer, about his company's priorities.

The successful entrepreneur will then look at the camera and lie...

You know, when we started Amazing Corporation 12 years ago, we just had one focus in mind: People. We knew if we only treated our people well, then the profits would take care of themselves.

Problem is, that's not what happened. Twelve years ago, this (even then totally boring) entrepreneur was swimming in debt. He had investors and banks calling him at all hours of the night asking for their money back. He never slept. And when he did, it was curled up in the corner of his disaster of an office. Back then, his one and only goal in life was to answer this one question: *How am I going to make money—now?*

Twelve years later, under the influence of his own brilliance revisionist history, this entrepreneur leads all the new founders astray. And they believe him, for after all, he is the (now totally boring and ridiculously rich) founder of Amazing Corporation.

I know you are going to ask so here goes: I believe in people. I honor the work they do and I'm happy to compensate them well for a day of hard work. That said, I am also acutely aware that the only reason I can pay them is because of the profit that's coming in through the front door.

No profit = No people.

So keep your eye on the numbers. Build a great company that makes money and delivers value.

Then build your team. Third.

Start with a competent operator. Someone who's done this before (in your industry) and have them build the infrastructure under them (not you). If you're the owner (and I am assuming for this example that you are), you have more important things to do than posting job openings and screening applicants.

Do these things and you will (as Spock once said) "live long and prosper."

Another 21-Day Business Miracle you might try is creating some kind of system in your business. Every great business should have—at a minimum—the following:

- A sales system.
- A lead generation system.
- A marketing system.
- A training product or service delivery system.
- A customer support system.
- A social media system.
- A hiring and training system.

That list is not exhaustive, but it is required. And here's what I mean by a "system." Let's take customer support. If your customer support system is *talk to my assistant Bertha* you don't have a system. If your system can get sick and take a week off, it's not a system. If your system can take another job, it's not a system.

A system means that everything is encapsulated in an SOP (standard operating procedure) that anyone can pick up and run with. A real system means that Bertha can take her mobile home to Yosemite for 3 weeks without internet and you'll be good.

Just take the time right now and figure out what audacious goal you want to accomplish or what systems you want to put in place. Then build your 21-Day Business Miracle to make it happen. The world needs your solution. And it's high time you did everything in your power to get it to them.

The 21-Day Addiction Miracle

> ***Disclaimer**: I am not a counselor or a doctor. I haven't gone to school to study addiction and I don't have a degree in therapy. I have, however, lost a brother to drugs. I have also successfully conquered a few addictions myself. I have some "in the trenches" experience I'd like to share, but nothing here constitutes medical or therapeutic advice. If you have a serious addiction, you may want to talk to a doctor. Or not. At the risk of sounding like a gigantic turd, it seems to me that "modern medicine" has addicted more people than it has liberated. Either way, it's time to get yourself free, so read on. You may just find the key to whatever door is holding you back.*

The first thing to know is that there are way more addictions than you can possibly imagine. When people talk about addiction, they are usually thinking of alcohol, drugs, cigarettes, or sex. It's been my experience that it's the other addictions that can really crush you. You see, everyone knows that drugs are a bad thing and they're easy to spot. Same for smoking. The problem with the other addictions is that they actually look "good on the outside," but they consume you on the inside.

Take, for example, the addiction to people's opinions. If that's an issue for you, you can easily turn your people-pleasing into fake kindness and cover it over for years—or forever. Your friends may even laud you for *how much you care* and you'll get showered with praise while deep down inside you're a total slave to public opinion. It looks good on the outside and it's reinforced emotionally which means it's that much harder to extricate.

But not to fear. If you want to take a good ax to the power of addiction, a 21-Day Addiction Miracle might just do the trick.

We return, once again, to the 21-Day Miracle 3-Step Process we outlined in Part I.

First, state your desired result. Let's use alcohol as an example...

I am totally and completely free from being addicted to alcohol.

Then, associate a strong emotion to your desired result.

- I am totally and completely free from being addicted to alcohol.
- I move through social situations with ease and have total control over my impulses.
- I imagine myself at a party and I realize that I am perfectly at ease not drinking. In fact, I like it better this way. (visual)
- My friends and family tell me they are amazed that I've gained so much control. (auditory)
- I feel free for the first time in my life. (kinesthetic)

Finally, create the plan and take action.

The first and most obvious thing to do during your 21-Day Addiction Miracle is the most obvious: **don't do whatever you used to be addicted to.** Just don't. If my story is anything like yours, the actual physical addiction will completely go away in about three days.

After that, what's left is an emotional or situational addiction. To overcome that, just stay away from the places where you have an emotional connection to the old habit. If you usually smoke on the golf course, then quit golfing for a few weeks. If you can't open your computer at night without looking at naked people, then don't open your computer at night.

Just remember, you don't have to do it for three weeks. You just have to do it for today. Tomorrow is a new day and you don't need to think about that right now. Breaking addiction is way easier when you know it's a short run. For the first week, pretend you're going to go back to it—and that you're just taking a few weeks off to cleanse your lungs, mind, mouth, whatever.

As you get halfway, you'll start replacing the good feeling of the addiction with the good feeling of achieving your goal. Then, you'll notice that what you are experiencing is the real thing and the addiction isn't even an addiction anymore.

Then, you'll be free.

One thing that helps is to replace the old habit with something similar—only positive. For example, I have completely quit caffeine several times and even now I drink mostly decaf. To do that, I first replaced coffee with naturally decaffeinated herbal tea or decaffeinated coffee. That little **"Replacement Hack"** tricks your brain and gives your hands something to do.

Last thing, one of the biggest lies in the addiction-recovery business is that there are two stages to overcoming addiction.

1. You want to do what you're addicted to and you **do**.

2. You want to do what you're addicted to and you **don't**.

But there is actually a third and very critical stage:

3. You don't want to do it anymore.

That means if you're addicted to alcohol, you should get to the point where you can go to a party and the thought of drinking never even crosses your mind.

Remember, Hive-Minded Lemmings do whatever their little brains tell them to do with little or no control. You're not a Hive-Minded Lemming and you're meant to change the world. So get on with your 21-Day Addiction Miracle so you can free your mind to accomplish your great and noble mission.

It may be easier than you think.

How to Keep What You've Earned

Congrats. You made it.

Most people don't read. And most people never get to the end of what they started. Most people are Hive-Minded Lemmings and you apparently aren't one of those.

Well done.

As we near the end, I want to show you how to keep everything that you earned from your 21-Day Miracle. When you dedicate 3-weeks to creating a new habit, you have something real that you can keep forever. So let's make sure it stays that way.

Upon completion of your 21-Day Miracle you have two very important things to do immediately. But chill because both will be easy.

First, celebrate. Have a blast. Throw a party. Tell everyone on social media how amazing you are. Do it. Not only do you deserve it, but celebration will solidify the new, positive habit.

Second, and this is very important, make sure you give yourself a break. Take at least one week off before you start another 21-Day Miracle. This might be a bit tempting because when your first 3 weeks is over, you're going to feel like you can climb any mountain and conquer any foe. And you're right. You can. Just after a short rest.

Earlier in the book, I said the 21-Day Miracle was patterned after nature that "grows in fits and starts, sprints and stops, struggle and rest." You just spent a full three weeks sprinting. Now take at least one week off to rest.

Sure, go ahead and plan, scheme, and think of new ideas. Heck, maybe even read this book again. But whatever you do, don't kick off anything big—at least not yet.

You made great strides in a very short time and you should be proud. What's not so proud is that old habit of yours. He just went into the corner to sulk. He just lost a lot of ground and will want to get back. The good news is the "keeping what you have" part is far easier than the sprint, but you still have to think about a few things.

First, any sustained activity in the other direction will solidify a new (and possibly bad) habit. So, for example, let's say you took 21-Days to get your relationships in line. You made a list, did a great job pruning, and you grew one significant relationship. You're thrilled and you feel really free and in love for the first time in your life.

Then, slowly, you let some things slip. And eventually, you're spending more and more time with those horrible, destructive people you eliminated in The 21-Day Relationship Miracle. After three weeks of hanging with that crowd, you'll be right back where you started.

That's because the 21-Day Miracle will work in whatever direction you choose. It's a powerful tool, but it's also obedient. If you use it to ruin your life, it will.

But like I said earlier, "keeping what you have" is far easier than the sprint, so you should be good. Just keep your eyes open and occasionally take stock of any new habits or beliefs that may have accidentally gotten in. Sometimes it's even worth a short 3-7 Day sprint to reinforce your good new habit.

You probably figured this out already, but you can use a 21-Day Miracle to do almost anything. I purposely chose 10 of the most common subjects to cover in this book. But there are probably more like 1,000 to choose from in real life. Once you know what you want to change, the process is simple...

- **State your desired result.**
- **Associate a strong emotion to your desired result.**
- **Create your plan and take action.**

Last thing, stay connected. Thousands of people are reading this book which means there are a lot of positive people like you out there.

Why not get together and change the world?

The discussion continues at...

www.EdRush.com/Bonus

Part III—Appendices

Appendix A—16 Rules To Change the World

Here is something I wrote as a set of rules for myself. I thought it might be useful, if for nothing else than to show you a new way of thinking. My recommendation is to print out a copy and post it somewhere prominent. You can find a PDF version on my website at www.EdRush.com/Bonus.

Most people aren't keen on rules. That's because most rules tell us what we *can't* do.

But what if I showed you a list of rules that gave you *more* freedom, space, and creativity? **What if I showed you a list of rules that could change the world?**

That's exactly what's below.

Global Rules

1. The world is an abundant place. There is an abundance of energy, money, water, ideas, resources, innovation, and people. The moment someone starts saying we don't have enough of "X" or that we are running out of "Y" is the moment to say "thank you for sharing" and move on.

2. The world's problems can NOT be solved by the world's governments. They move too slowly and think slower still. Solving big problems requires an entrepreneurial mind, a commitment to agility, and the willingness to risk. Of these three, governments possess none.

3. People should be compensated for the value they provide, not for the years they have worked.

4. Markets always catch up. You can bend, manipulate, coerce, and hide. Eventually the market will catch up. If you want to make a lot of money,

innovate in a market that is manipulated and controlled by bureaucracy. Examples—mortgage shorts in 2008, Uber vs. taxi lobby, and any industry that has excessive regulation.

5. In 30 years, the world will be ruled by the countries that make the fastest decisions, not by the ones with the biggest guns. Example—North Korea has big guns, sketchy WiFi, and no one goes there on vacation.

6. Change in the free market creates opportunity. Opportunity (once capitalized on) creates wealth. If you live in a country where it is legally, religiously, or competitively impossible to go from broke to billionaire in a year, then move. Now.

7. In an entrepreneurial world, more people means more resources. Thus, population growth is a *good* thing. That's because entrepreneurs create more than they consume. If you're an entrepreneur, have babies.

8. Within 25 years, automation will have completely eliminated the following jobs:

a. Financial advisors (sorry, not sorry)

b. Real estate agents (6%, 5%, 4%...)

c. Drivers of any kind (limo, truckers, train conductors, etc... This list also includes Uber drivers, and the chain-smoking taxi driver)

d. Airline pilots (planes have been flown by computers for at least 20 years so nothing new here)

e. Dry cleaners (drop your shirt in a box, come back in 10 mins, done. BTW—create this and I might just fund you.)

f. Janitors (Think Roomba)

g. Window cleaners (Think Vertical Roomba)

h. Printers (I give this one 10 years. My bet is that the "everyday" printer will close his shop and start driving for Uber, only to be replaced by another driverless Uber car 10 years later. Don't be everyday. Don't.)

NOTE—If your job is on this list, it's time to find a new career that isn't going to be taken over by a computer. If your job is not on this list, but you steadily complain that your job is being commoditized and sent overseas, it's also time to find a new career—a new attitude—or both.

Personal Rules

1. **Time** is the most valuable asset on earth. You can take away my house, my car, my savings, my IRA, my investments, my boat, and my wallet. I can get them all back. But if you take away one minute of my time, it's gone. Forever. So, I choose to be wise with my time and to honor other people's time. It's precious.

2. Money is neither good nor bad. Money is amoral. For an evil man, money is gained immorally and used for evil. For a good man, money is gained morally and used for good. I will choose to be a good man, earning

money in a good way to use for good ends.

3. I choose not to ride anyone else's roller coaster. Friends, bosses, spouses, colleagues, and clients will all go up and down. One minute happy; the next minute sad. One day hopeful; the day hopeless. One week optimistic; the next week pessimistic. They have chosen to ride their own roller coaster —and often without any tangible reason as to why. It's my choice to get on. So I choose not to.

4. I am, by rule, willing to say no to anyone at any time for any reason without a sentence being required after the word "no." And not to be a jerk. It's because when I say "yes" to one thing I say "no" to something else. So we're not getting together so you can "pick my brain."

5. I am not morally obligated to respond to every email or text message any more than I am required to respond to every billboard. This

goes double if you just happened to guess my email address.

6. Failure is a GIFT. It is a precious indication that I have veered off target. I choose, then, to see failure as a sign pointing to a much-needed correction. For every one success, I have had ten failures. Thank you, failure.

7. Criticism is also a GIFT. It means I am onto something. If a critical person reads a brilliant article, his critical brain will require him to find a spelling error. If a critical person reads drivel, he says nothing. Thank you, criticism.

8. If someone's rule starts with "here's why I can't do this…" it's a bogus, made-up rule that is worth tossing out the window at the first opportunity. If their rule starts with "that's impossible because…" then it's worth throwing out the window, backing up, and driving over it a few times—just to be sure.

I'd love to hear any rules you live by or how this list helped you.

Appendix B: The 21-Day Miracle Plans

Welcome to The 21-Day Miracle Plans! You're fired up and ready to go and these outlines will help you create a plan and get started.

A few notes:

1. I wrote these plans for independent thinkers and not Hive-Minded Lemmings. That means everything is an example and not a "To Do List." So as you study the Plans, be sure to be creative and make your own version that works for you.

2. I created a series of PDFs for each plan. That way, you can print out the Plan that works for you and get started. You can get those on the Plans section at the Free Training Site...

www.EdRush.com/Bonus

3. If you skipped ahead to this section without reading any of the book, you're about to be very confused. Do yourself a favor and read Part I of the book.

21-Day Miracle Implementation Plans

The 21-Day Mind Mastery Miracle Plan

State your desired result.

Example:
I have total mastery over my mind.

Associate a strong emotion to your desired result.

Example:

- I have total mastery over my mind.
- My thoughts are mine and I only dwell on the things I choose to dwell on.
- Stress and fear are gone. In their place are joy, happiness, and security.
- I use my mind to create amazing things in my life and business.
- I see many people coming to hear and listen to me because of my wisdom. (visual)
- My friends and family keep telling me how much I have changed. (auditory)

- I feel free for the first time in my life. (kinesthetic)

Create your plan and take action.

Step #1: Awareness and Observation

Spend a minimum of 10 minutes a day for one week doing nothing more than observing your thoughts.

Step #2: Eliminate and Replace

Armed with a good understanding of your thought patterns, on Day #8, write a list of all of the negative thoughts you have been believing.

Then make a new list of the positive thoughts you're going to replace the negative thoughts with.

Example:

Negative thought: *I hate the way my body looks.*
Positive thought: *I am fearfully and wonderfully made, that my body is a gift, and I love looking at what I see.*

Then format a new statement using the format below:

I reject the lie that ________ (insert negative statement) and I choose to believe that ________ (insert positive statement).

Example:
I reject the lie that I am unhappy with my body. I choose instead to believe that I am fearfully and wonderfully made, that my body is a gift, and I love looking at what I see.

Do that every day for 21-Days.

The 21-Day Mind Mastery Miracle Plan Worksheet

State your desired result.

(Insert 1 line here)

Associate a strong emotion to your desired result.

(insert about 6 lines here)

Create your plan and take action.

Step #1: Awareness and Observation

(Insert 2 lines here)

Step #2: Eliminate and Replace

Negative thought:
(Insert 1 line here)

Positive (replacement) thought:
(Insert 1 line here)

New Statement:
I reject the lie that

____

____

____

____

(insert negative statement)
and I choose to believe that

____

____

____

____

(insert positive statement).

The 21-Day Money Mastery Miracle Plan

State your desired result.

Example:
I have total mastery over money.

Associate a strong emotion to your desired result.

Example:

- I have total mastery over my money.
- Money flows quickly and easily to me from multiple sources.
- I see myself with total financial freedom. (visual)
- I hear people asking each other how I was able to do it so quickly. (auditory)
- I take a big breath and relax because I now have the resources help a lot of people. (kinesthetic)

Create your plan and take action.

Step #1: Awareness and Observation

Spend a minimum of 10 minutes a day for one week doing nothing more than observing your thoughts about money.

Spend some of that time imagining an extremely wealthy person. Imagine everything you can about their lifestyle. Take note of any negative thoughts and emotions that come up.

Ask yourself your view on money. Is money good, evil, or neither?

Step #2: Eliminate and Replace

Armed with a good understanding of your thought patterns, write a list of all of the negative thoughts you have been believing about money.

Then make a new list of the positive thoughts you're going to replace them with.

Example:

Negative thought: *Money is evil.*
Positive thought: *Money is neither good nor bad. So I choose to be a good rich person who uses money to do good things.*

Then format a new statement using the format below:

I reject the lie that ________(insert negative statement about money) and I choose to believe that ________(insert positive statement about money).

Example:
I reject the lie that money is evil and I choose instead to believe that money is neither good nor bad. So I choose to be a good rich person who uses money to do good things.

Do that for 21-Days.

Finally, write down a list of the things you do that bring you the most money.

Focus on doing at least one of those things every day for 21 days.

The 21-Day Money Mastery Miracle Plan Worksheet

State your desired result.

(Insert 1 line here)

Associate a strong emotion to your desired result.

(insert about 6 lines here)

Create your plan and take action.

Step #1: Awareness and Observation

(Insert 2 lines here)

Step #2: Eliminate and Replace

Negative thought:
(Insert 1 line here)

Positive (replacement) thought:
(Insert 1 line here)

New Statement:
I reject the lie that

____

____

____

____

(insert negative statement)
and I choose to believe that

____

____

____

____

(insert positive statement).

Money Making Activities

What activities do you participate in that are always money-making?

(Insert 6 lines here)

Every work day, for 21 days, do one of the activities above.

The 21-Day Inner Warrior Miracle Plan

State your desired result.

Example:
I am a warrior. I stand up for what's right and no one can stop me.

Associate a strong emotion to your desired result.

Example:

- I am a warrior. I stand up for what's right and no one can stop me.
- I am a man.[102]
- I think, act, and behave like a man. That means I use my strength to serve those who need it most and to create great value in the world.
- I see myself as a Gladiator, fighting to set people free. (visual)
- I hear the crowd roar and know they, too, believe in something greater. (auditory)

- I feel amazing because I am finally the man I was meant to be. (kinesthetic)

Create your plan and take action.

Step #1: Purposeful Intake

Make a list of the things that you are going to watch, read, and listen to over the next 21-days.

That list includes...

- Movies / TV
- Books
- Music
- Podcasts

Make that list on Day #1 and create a plan for your 21-Day intake.

Step #2: Take Purposeful Risks

At least once, over the next 21 days, you will stand up for someone or something that needs standing up for.

Just keep your eyes open. It will happen.

The 21-Day Inner Warrior Plan Worksheet

State your desired result.

(Insert 1 line here)

Associate a strong emotion to your desired result.

(insert about 6 lines here)

Create your plan and take action.

Step #1: Purposeful Intake

Movies / TV
(Insert 2 lines here)

Books
(Insert 2 lines here)

Music

(Insert 2 lines here)

Podcasts

(Insert 2 lines here)

Step #2: Take Purposeful Risks

Write here what you did and how you felt.

(Insert lines here to end of page)

The 21-Day Time Freedom Miracle Plan

State your desired result.

Example:
I am in charge of my time and my schedule.

Associate a strong emotion to your desired result.

Example:

- I am in charge of my time and my schedule.
- I have the perfect mix of work, leisure, and family time.
- I choose to only do the most profitable tasks.
- I see myself sitting outside at the end of a very productive day while I read a book and enjoy the sunshine. (visual)
- People keep telling me they can't believe how much I can get done in so little time. (auditory)

- I feel free for the first time in my life and I plan to keep it this way. (kinesthetic)

Create your plan and take action.

Option #1: Create a structure for your life that effectively manages people, technology, and yourself.

Some examples:

- Set one weekly meeting with key team members instead of allowing them access all day long.
- Create a set of rules that limits when you will check email.
- Schedule time every day for PDT (personal development time).

Pick one or two and do it for 21 work days.

Option #2: Calculate the Value of Your Time.

Take an average workweek of 40 hours.
Multiply it by the number of weeks in a year (round to 50).
That gives you a round 2,000 hours of "work time" per year.

Now, simply divide 2,000 into your income goal and you'll instantly discover what each hour is worth.

If you want to make $100,000 a year, your time-value is $50 / hour.
If you want to make $1,000,000 a year, your time-value is $500 / hour.

Insert Your Time Value:

____

Now create a plan to get that dollar figure out of each hour of every work day.

Option #3: "Script" Your Work Days.

I recommend scripting them out like a movie director. Each day, for 21-Days, do the following:

7. First, make a list of the things you want to accomplish. (note—this "to do list" is as far as most people go.)
8. Assign a priority to each task—from 1 to 10.
9. Assign a time to each task—from 10 minutes to 8 hours.
10. Then, script out the hours of your day starting with the highest priority tasks all the way to the lowest.
11. Start your first task and set a timer. {103} You're running against the clock. If you finish late, move faster next time. If you finish early, great. Take a break. Get coffee or check email.
12. Then start the clock again and get on to the next task.

Do that every work day for 21-Days.

The 21-Day Time Freedom Miracle Plan Worksheet

State your desired result.

(Insert 1 line here)

Associate a strong emotion to your desired result.

(insert about 6 lines here)

Create your plan and take action.

Create a structure for your life that effectively manages people, technology, and yourself.

People
(Insert 2 lines here)

Technology
(Insert 2 lines here)

Yourself
(Insert 2 lines here)

Calculate the Value of Your Time.

Insert Your Time Value:

____

My plan to maximize each hour to get my desired “time value”:
(Insert 5-6 lines here)

“Script” Your Work Days.

(Insert 6 lines here)

The 21-Day Life Balance Miracle Plan Worksheet

Sorry, this isn't going to happen.

Just be present each day and drive aggressively toward your family, life, or career dreams.

And read the super-short chapter in the book on this topic if you're totally confused right now.

The 21-Day Happiness Miracle Plan

State your desired result.

Example:
I am happy and full of joy despite my circumstances.

Associate a strong emotion to your desired result.

Example:

- I am happy and full of joy despite my circumstances.
- I picture myself smiling a lot. (visual)
- People compliment me because I have a lot of fun doing what I do. (auditory)
- I feel great because I control my happiness and I control my emotions. (kinesthetic)

Create your plan and take action.

Step #1: Awareness and Observation

Spend a minimum of ten minutes a day for one week doing nothing more than observing your “silly little roller coaster of emotion.” During that first week, take a good look at how you *feel* at several times during the day. Setting an hourly timer and keeping a journal helps.

Write down the negative emotions you are experiencing like sadness, anger, frustration, etc.

Step #2: Eliminate and Replace Old Emotions (With These “Back Door” Brain Hacks)

Every day, for the remaining 21-Days execute one of these “Back Door Brain Hacks”:

- **“I Feel Amazing!”**
- **Rock Your Energy**
- **The Gorilla**
- **The Gratitude Hack**
- **The Present Minded Meal**

The 21-Day Happiness Miracle Plan Worksheet

State your desired result.

(Insert 1 line here)

Associate a strong emotion to your desired result.

(insert about 6 lines here)

Step #1: Awareness and Observation

What are the negative and unhelpful emotions you are experiencing?
(insert about 6 lines here)

Step #2: Eliminate and Replace Old Emotions (With "Back Door" Brain Hacks)

What “hack” are you going to use to “replace” the negative emotion when it comes up?
(insert about 6 lines here)

The 21-Day Body Miracle Plan

State your desired result.

Example:
I look great. I am at my ideal level of fitness and I eat healthy food that I love.

Associate a strong emotion to your desired result.

Example:

- I look great. I am at my ideal level of fitness and I eat healthy food that I love.
- I have renewed mastery over food. I love what I eat—it's good, healthy, and fresh.
- I follow a movement routine that makes me feel amazing.
- I look at myself in the mirror, and hey, I look great. (visual)

- I scream, "I feel great!" at the top of my lungs. I don't care who hears. (auditory)
- I feel confident in how I look and feel. (kinesthetic)

Create your plan and take action.

Feel free to do only one of the things below for 21-Days or mix and match.

Step #1: Food

For 21-Days, don't drink anything that has calories. The list of approved beverages includes: water, sparkling water, coffee, and tea. (Or anything else that has no calories and no sugar.)

Or

For 21 days, only eat food that is 100% organic, gluten-free, dairy-free, and sugar-free.

Step #2: Movement

Every day, for 21-Days[104] do one of the following activities...

- Biking
- Basketball, Baseball, Softball, or anything else that ends with the word "ball."
- Boxing. Wrestling. Jiu Jitsu.
- Running. Walking.
- Hiking.
- Yard Work / Manual Labor.
- Functional Weight Lifting.
- Yoga. Stretching.

The 21-Day Body Miracle Plan Worksheet

State your desired result.

(Insert 1 line here)

Associate a strong emotion to your desired result.

(insert about 6 lines here)

Step #1: Food

Insert your food plan here...
(insert about 6 lines here)

Step #2: Movement

For 21-Days I am going to do one of the following activities...
(insert about 6 lines here)

The 21-Day Relationship Miracle Plan

State your desired result.

Example:
I have uplifting relationships filled with love and empathy, and I am protected by proper boundaries.

Associate a strong emotion to your desired result.

Example:

- I have uplifting relationships filled with love and empathy, and I am protected by proper boundaries.
- I only spend time with people who are a blessing to me.
- I only spend time with people I bless.
- I picture all my family members enjoying time with me. (visual)
- They keep telling me how thankful they are that we are together. (auditory)

- I feel so connected and fulfilled. (kinesthetic)

Create your plan and take action.

Step #1: Evaluate Your Relationships

Using the contacts on your phone, make a list of all the relationships in your life. Give everyone a score.

1—This person makes your life harder, is difficult to be around, or steals energy from you. In other words, they are a gigantic pain in the posterior.
2—This person neither adds nor takes away from you. Neutral.
3—This person gives you more life and you love being around them.

Step #2: Prune Negative Relationships

Using the list in Step #1, take every person who scored a "1" and put them in one of two columns: **Eliminate** or **RTR (Re-Define the Relationship).**

Set a time to have a conversation with the people in the RTR column. Do that now. You're going to want to put this off. Just do it. You'll be glad you did.

Step#3: Grow Your Good Relationships

Every day, for 21-Days, spend just 10 minutes a day doing nothing more than *thinking* about someone you love. You don't even have to do anything for them. Just find a comfortable, quiet place, start your timer, and imagine what it's like to be them. Do that. Close your eyes and imagine that you are, in fact, them.

- What were they thinking about when they went to bed last night?
- What did they feel like when they woke up this morning?
- What are they thinking about now?

- What's a big priority for them this month?
- If they could go anywhere on a vacation right now, where would it be?
- What books are they reading?
- What movies have they been waiting to watch?
- What's the biggest challenge they are having in life?

The 21-Day Relationship Miracle Plan Worksheet

State your desired result.

(Insert 1 line here)

Associate a strong emotion to your desired result.

(insert about 6 lines here)

Create your plan and take action.

Step #1: Evaluate Your Relationships

"1"s
(insert about 3 lines here)

"2"s
(insert about 3 lines here)

"3"s

(insert about 3 lines here)

Step #2: Prune Negative Relationships

Re-write the "1"s and next to each one write **Eliminate** or **RTR (Re-Define the Relationship).** Set a deadline for the RTR's.
(insert about 6 lines here)

Step#3: Grow Your Good Relationships

What did you notice when you spent 10 minutes thinking about one of your "3"s?
(insert about 6 lines here)

The 21-Day Business Miracle Plan

State your desired result.

Example:
I have written a book, created a website, and launched a training product called the 21-Day Miracle.

Associate a strong emotion to your desired result.

Example:

- In 3 short weeks, I have written a book, created a website, and launched a training product called the 21-Day Miracle.
- The wisdom I share will help millions of people change their lives and the world.
- I picture the people helped by this message and I smile. (visual)

• People keep telling me how much they've learned and grown through the 21-Day Miracle. (auditory)
• I feel amazing because I created great value in my business and helped so many people. (kinesthetic)

Create your plan and take action.

Option #1: Create Positioning and Authority

Chose one from the following list or write another activity that creates positioning or authority:

- **Write a book.**
- **Launch an interview show or podcast.**
- **Speak.**
- **Write** blogs, LinkedIn Publisher articles, Facebook posts, articles in trade journals or news outlet.
- **Create videos** for YouTube or your website.

Option #2: Get and Close Deals

Set aside one full, un-interrupted hour a day to do whatever activity gets you more deals, leads, and customers.

Option #3: Build a Team and Infrastructure to Support #1 and #2

Every day, for 21-Days, spend one hour a day building or supporting a team and infrastructure to get you better positioning and customers.

Option #4: Create Systems

Every work day for 21-Days, dedicate at least one hour a day to creating one of the following...

- A sales system.
- A lead generation system.
- A marketing system.

- A training product or service delivery system.
- A customer support system.
- A social media system.
- A hiring and training system.

The 21-Day Business Miracle Plan Worksheet

State your desired result.

(Insert 1 line here)

Associate a strong emotion to your desired result.

(insert about 6 lines here)

Create your plan and take action.

Option #1: Create Positioning and Authority

Write down the one thing you're going to do over the next three weeks to better position you as an authority in your marketplace. Then write down when are you going to do it—with a deadline.
(insert about 3 lines here)

Option #2: Get and Close Deals

Write down what you're going to do for one full, un-interrupted hour a day to get more deals, leads, and customers. Then write down when are you going to do it—with a deadline.
(insert about 6 lines here)

Option #3: Build a Team and Infrastructure to Support #1 and #2

Write down what you're going to do to build or support a team and infrastructure to get you better positioning and customers.
(insert about 6 lines here)

Option #4: Create Systems

Write down what you're going to do to create better systems in your business.
(insert about 6 lines here)

The 21-Day Addiction-Breaking Miracle Plan

State your desired result.

Example:
I am totally and completely free from being addicted to alcohol.

Associate a strong emotion to your desired result.

Example:

- I am totally and completely free from being addicted to alcohol.
- I move through social situations with ease and have total control over my impulses.
- I imagine myself at a party and I realize that I am perfectly at ease not drinking. In fact, I like it better this way. (visual)
- My friends and family tell me they are amazed that I've gained so much control. (auditory)

- I feel free for the first time in my life. (kinesthetic)

Create your plan and take action.

Step #1: Don't do the thing to which you are addicted

Write down the negative activity and then just don't do it for 21-days.

Step #2: Replace The Negative Habit with a Positive Habit

Write down your replacement to the negative activity.

The 21-Day Addiction-Breaking Miracle Plan Worksheet

State your desired result.

(Insert 1 line here)

Associate a strong emotion to your desired result.

(insert about 6 lines here)

Create your plan and take action.

Step #1: Don't do the thing to which you are addicted

Write down your negative activity.
(insert about 3 lines here)

Step #2: Replace The Negative Habit with a Positive Habit

Write down your replacement to the negative activity.
(insert about 3 lines here)

Hiring Ed to Speak

Hey there! It's Ed again. If you host events (or know someone who does), let's talk. One of my passions is speaking and I'd love to bring a fun message of inspiration to your corporation, association, group, or church. Of note, I do this as a business, so I am not coming to Milwaukee because it's "the right thing to do." But if you have a *real* budget and you want to hire a *real* speaker, let's talk.

The office number is 619-292-2599 and direct email is support@EdRush.com. If you get the recording, be sure to leave the date of the meeting and budget for your event.

Hiring Ed for Consulting

One of the fastest ways to explode your business is by getting advice from someone who has been there and done that.

Like Liam Neeson in *Taken*, I have "a particular skill." Only in this case, my particular skill is showing business owners how to make more and work less. Most entrepreneurs do about 100 things and feel guilty about the other 100 things they aren't doing. By the time we're done, you'll have 2-4 things that drive all your revenue. And you'll have way more peace of mind.

I am ridiculously expensive and you probably can't afford me. But for the right business, what I know might just work miracles for your bottom line.

Some of the things we could work on together include...

- Lead generation & follow up
- Mobile marketing
- Facebook marketing
- Content creation
- Funnel creation
- Speaking
- Pitching & closing more deals
- How to do your own live or virtual events

- Trade show and live event lead generation and sales
- Facebook Live, YouTube Live, livestreaming, webcasts and webinars
- How to present and perform on video
- Interviewing strategies
- Celebrity branding strategies
- Product creation
- Podcasting
- Publicity and getting booked on media
- Book publishing
- Marketing automation
- Outsourcing
- Creating systems in your business for marketing, sales, customer support, and more.

This list is not exhaustive. You might just want to hire me to come up with a 12-month plan to double your revenue.

CPSIA information can be obtained
at www.ICGtesting.com
Printed in the USA
LVHW022112210423
745008LV00003B/425

9 781806 311903